RULERS O

LORD CLIVE

BY COLONEL G. B. MALLESON

PREFACE

The following list represents the works of the last century which I have consulted to write this *Life of Lord Clive:*

Orme's *History of Indostan* (original edition); *The Siyaru-l Muta-akherin* of Ghulám Husain Khán (Review of Modern Times), translated copy; Cambridge's *War in India* (containing the Journal of Stringer Lawrence); *The Memoir of Dupleix* (in French); Grose's *Voyage to the East Indies;* Ive's *Voyage and Historical Narrative; Transactions in India from the commencement of the French War in 1756* (published in 1786); Caraccioli's *Life of Lord Clive;* Vansittart's *Narrative of the Transactions in Bengal;* Ironside's *Narrative of the Military Transactions in Bengal in 1760-1;* Verelst's *English Government in Bengal;* some numbers of the *Asiatic Annual Register;* Kindersley's *Letters;* and Scrafton's *Letters;* and, for the earlier period—that displaying the period immediately preceding and following the dawn of genius—the recently written extracts from the Madras records by Mr. G. W. Forrest.

Of works of scarcely less value published during the present century, I have consulted the admirable volumes by Colonel Mark Wilks, which bring the *History of Southern India* down to the storming of Seringapatam in 1799; *The Journal of Captain Dalton,* one of the heroes of Trichinopoli, written at the period of Clive's early victories, but only given to the world, with a memoir of his career, in 1886; Lord Stanhope's *History of England;* Malcolm's *Life of Clive,* and above all, that mine of wealth to a searcher into the details of Clive's services in Bengal, Colonel Broome's *History of the Bengal Army.* Colonel Broome was my intimate and valued friend. He knew more about the history of the rise of the English in India than any man I ever met. He had made the subject a life-study. He had read every tract, however old, every letter, however difficult to decipher, every record of the period up to and beyond the time of Job Charnock, and he was a past-master of his subject. He had collected an enormous mass of materials, the more bulky of which were dispersed at his untimely death. But I have seen and handled them, and I can state most positively, from my own knowledge, that every item of importance culled from them is contained in the admirable volume to which I have referred, and which was published in 1850. There is, alas, only that volume. Colonel Broome had set apart a vast mass of materials for his second, and had resolved to complete the work at Simla, to which place he was proceeding for the summer of, I think, 1870. But, in the course of transit, the box containing the materials was mysteriously spirited away, and I have not heard that it was ever found. From the nature of the documents collected I cannot but regard the loss as irreparable.

G. B. MALLESON.

NOTE

The orthography of proper names follows the system adopted by the Indian Government for the *Imperial Gazetteer of India.* That system, while adhering to the popular spelling of very well-known places, such as Punjab, Poona, Deccan, &c., employs in all other cases the vowels with the following uniform sounds:—

a, as in wom*a*n: *á,* as in f*a*ther: *i,* as in k*i*n: *í,* as in intr*i*gue: *o,* as in c*o*ld: *u,* as in b*u*ll: *ú,* as in r*u*ral.

LORD CLIVE

CHAPTER I
EARLY YEARS

Towards the close of the year 1744 there landed at Madras, as writer in the service of the East India Company, a young Englishman just entering the twentieth year of his existence, named Robert Clive.

The earlier years of the life of this young man had not been promising. Born at Styche, near Market Drayton, in Shropshire, he had been sent, when three years old, to be cared for and educated at Manchester, by a gentleman who had married his mother's sister, Mr. Bayley of Hope Hall. The reason for this arrangement, at an age so tender, is not known. One seeks for it in vain in the conduct and character of his parents; for although his father is described as irascible and violent, his mother was remarkable for her good sense and sweet temper. To her, Clive was wont to say, he owed more than to all his schools. But he could have seen but little of her in those early days, for his home was always with the Bayleys, even after the death of Mr. Bayley, and he was ever treated there with kindness and consideration. After one or two severe illnesses, which, it is said, affected his constitution in after life, the young Robert, still of tender years, was sent to Dr. Eaton's private school at Lostocke in Cheshire: thence, at eleven, he was removed to Mr. Burslem's at Market Drayton. With this gentleman he remained a few years, and was then sent to have a brief experience of a public school at Merchant Taylors'. Finally, he went to study at a private school kept by Mr. Sterling in Hertfordshire. There he remained until, in 1743, he was nominated to be a writer in the service of the East India Company.

The chief characteristics of Robert Clive at his several schools had been boldness and insubordination. He would not learn; he belonged to a 'fighting caste'; he was the leader in all the broils and escapades of schoolboy life; the terror of the masters; the spoiled darling of his schoolmates. He learned, at all events, how to lead: for he was daring even to recklessness; never lost his head; was calmest when the danger was greatest; and displayed in a hundred ways his predilection for a career of action.

It is not surprising, then, that he showed the strongest aversion to devote himself to the study which would have qualified him to follow his father's profession. A seat at an attorney's desk, and the drudgery of an attorney's life, were to him as distasteful as they proved to be, at a later period, to the eldest son of Isaac Disraeli. He would have a career which promised action. If such were not open to him in his native land, he would seek for it in other parts of the world. When, then, his father, who had some interest, and who had but small belief in his eldest son, procured for him the appointment of writer in the service of the East India Company, Robert Clive accepted it with avidity.

Probably if he had had the smallest idea of the nature of the duties which were associated with that office, he would have refused it with scorn. He panted, I have said, for a life of action: he accepted a career which was drudgery under a tropical sun, in its most uninteresting form. The Company in whose service he entered was simply a trading corporation. Its territory in India consisted of but a few square miles round the factories its agents had established, and for which they paid an annual rental to the native governments. They had but a small force, composed principally of the children of the soil, insufficiently armed, whose chief duties were escort duties and the manning of the ill-constructed forts which protected the Company's warehouses. The idea of aggressive warfare had never entered the heads even of the boldest of the English agents. They recognized the native ruler of the province in which lay their factories as their overlord, and they were content to hold their lands from him on the condition of protection on his part, and of good behaviour and punctual payment of rent on their own. For the combative energies of a young man such as

Robert Clive there was absolutely no field on Indian soil. The duties devolving on a writer were the duties of a clerk; to keep accounts; to take stock; to make advances; to ship cargoes; to see that no infringement of the Company's monopoly should occur. He was poorly paid; his life was a life of dull routine; and, although after many years of toil the senior clerks were sometimes permitted to trade on their own account and thus to make large fortunes, the opportunity rarely came until after many years of continuous suffering, and then generally when the climate had exhausted the man's energies.

To a young man of the nature of Robert Clive such a life could not be congenial. And, in fact, he hated it from the outset. He had left England early in 1743; his voyage had been long and tiring: the ship on which he sailed had put in at Rio, and was detained there nine months; it remained anchored for a shorter period in St. Simon's Bay; and finally reached Madras only at the close of 1744. The delays thus occurring completely exhausted the funds of the young writer: he was forced to borrow at heavy interest from the captain: the friend at Madras, to whom he had letters of introduction, had quitted that place. The solitary compensating advantage was this, that his stay at Rio had enabled him to pick up a smattering of Portuguese.

We see him, at length arrived, entering upon those hard and uninteresting duties to undertake which he had refused a life of far less drudgery in England in a congenial climate and under a sun more to be desired than dreaded. Cast loose in the profession he had selected, separated from relatives and friends, he had no choice but to enter upon the work allotted to him. This he did sullenly and with no enthusiasm. How painful was even this perfunctory performance; how keenly he felt the degradation—for such he deemed it— may be judged from the fact recorded by his contemporaries and accepted by the world, that for a long time he held aloof from his companions and his superiors. These in their turn ceased after a time to notice a young man so resolute to shun them. And although with time came an approach to intercourse, there never was cordiality. It is doubtful, however, whether in this description there has not mingled more than a grain of exaggeration. We have been told of his wayward nature: we have read how he insulted a superior functionary, and when ordered by the Governor to apologize, complied with the worst possible grace: how, when the pacified superior, wishing to heal the breach, asked him to dinner, he refused with the words that although the Governor had ordered him to apologize, he did not command him to dine with him: how, one day, weary of his monotonous existence, and suffering from impecuniosity, he twice snapped a loaded pistol at his head; how, on both occasions, there was a misfire; how, shortly afterwards, a companion, entering the room, at Clive's request pointed the pistol outside the window and pulled the trigger; how the powder ignited, and how then Clive, jumping to his feet, exclaimed, 'I feel I am reserved for better things.'

These stories have been told with an iteration which would seem to stamp them as beyond contradiction. But the publication of Mr. Forrest's records of the Madras Presidency (1890) presents a view altogether different. The reader must understand that the Board at Fort St. David—at that time the ruling Board in the Madras Presidency—is reporting, for transmission to Europe, an account of a complaint of assault made by the Rev. Mr. Fordyce against Clive.

It would appear from this that Mr. Fordyce was a coward and a bully, besides being in many other respects an utterly unfit member of society. It had come to Clive's ears that this man had said of him, in the presence of others, that he, Clive, was a coward and a scoundrel; that the reverend gentleman had shaken his cane over him in the presence of Mr. Levy Moses; and had told Captain Cope that he would break every bone in his (Clive's) skin. In his deposition Clive stated that these repeated abuses so irritated him, 'that he could not forbear, on meeting Mr. Fordyce at Cuddalore, to reproach him with his behaviour, which, he told him, was so injurious he could bear it no longer, and thereupon struck him two or three times with his cane, which, at last Mr. Fordyce returned and then closed in with him, but that they were presently parted by Captain Lucas.'

The Board, in giving its judgement on the case, recapitulated the many offences committed by Mr. Fordyce, the great provocation he had given to Clive, and suspended him. With regard to Clive they recorded: 'lest the same,' the attack on Fordyce, 'should be to Mr. Clive's prejudice, we think it not improper to assure you that he is generally esteemed a very quiet person and no ways guilty of disturbances.' It is to be inferred from this account that, far from deserving the character popularly assigned to him, Clive, in the third year of his residence in India, was regarded by his superiors as a very quiet member of society.

Still, neither the climate nor the profession suited him. 'I have not enjoyed,' he wrote to one of his cousins, 'a happy day since I left my native country.' In other letters he showed how he repented bitterly of having chosen a career so uncongenial. Gradually, however, he realized the folly of kicking against the pricks. He associated more freely with his colleagues, and when the Governor, Mr. Morse, sympathizing with the young man eating out his heart from ennui, opened to him the door of his considerable library, he found some relief to his sufferings. These, at last, had reached their term. Before Clive had exhausted all the books thus placed at his disposal, events occurred which speedily opened to him the career for which he had panted.

CHAPTER II
SOUTHERN INDIA IN 1744

It will contribute to the better understanding of the narrative of the events which plunged the English into war in 1745, if we take a bird's-eye view of the peninsula generally, particularly of the southern portion, as it appeared in the year preceding.

Of India generally it is sufficient to say that from the year 1707, when the Emperor Aurangzeb died, authority had been relaxing to an extent which was rapidly bringing about the disruption of the bonds that held society together. The invasion of Nadír Sháh followed by the sack of Delhi in 1739 had given the Mughal dynasty a blow from which it never rallied. Thenceforward until 1761, when the third battle of Pánípat completed the catastrophe, the anarchy was almost universal. Authority was to the strongest. The Sallustian motto, 'Alieni appetens sui profusus,' was the rule of almost every noble; the agriculturists had everywhere abundant reason to realize 'that the buffalo was to the man who held the bludgeon.'[1]

[1] The late Lord Lawrence used to tell me that when he was Acting Magistrate and Collector of Pánípat in 1836, the natives were in the habit of describing the lawlessness of the period which ceased in 1818 by using the expressive phrase I have quoted.

The disorder had extended to the part of India south of the Vindhyan range which was then known under the comprehensive term of the Deccan. When Aurangzeb had conquered many Súbahs, or provinces, of Southern India, he had placed them under one officer, to be nominated by the Court of Delhi, and to be called Súbahdár, or chief of the province. As disorder spread after his death the Súbahdárs and inferior chiefs generally began to secure themselves in the provinces they administered. The invasion of Nadír Sháh made the task generally easy. In the Deccan especially, Chin Kílich Khán, the chief of a family which had served with consideration under Akbar and his successors, whose father had been a favourite of Aurangzeb, who had himself served under that sovereign, and who had obtained from the successors of Aurangzeb the titles of Nizám-ul-Múlk and Asaf Jáh, took steps to make the Súbahdárship of Southern India hereditary in his family. The territories comprehended under the term 'Deccan' did not, it must be understood, include the whole of Southern India. Mysore, Travancore, Cochin were independent. But they comprehended the whole of the territories known now as appertaining to the Nizám, with some additions; the country known as the 'Northern Circárs'; and the Karnátik.

But the Karnátik was not immediately under the government of the Súbahdár. It was a subordinate territory, entrusted to a Nawáb, bounded to the north by the river Gundlakamma; on the west by the chain of mountains which separate it from Mysore; to the south by the possessions of the same kingdom (as it then was) and by Tanjore; to the east by the sea. I have not mentioned the kingdom of Trichinopoli to the south, for the Nawábs of the Karnátik claimed that as their own, and, as we shall see, had occupied the fortress of that name during the period, prior to 1744, of which I am writing.

It will be seen then, that, at this period, whilst the nominal ruler of the Deccan was Chin Kílich Khán, better known as Nizám-ul-Múlk, as I shall hereafter style him, the Nawáb of the Karnátik, who ruled the lands bordering on the sea, including the English settlement of Madras and the French settlement of Pondicherry, was a very powerful subordinate. The office he held had likewise come to be regarded as hereditary. And it was through the failure of the hereditary line, that the troubles came, which gave to Robert Clive the opportunity to develop the qualities which lay dormant within him.

Before I proceed to describe those events, it seems advisable to say a few words regarding the two settlements to which I have just referred; of the principles which actuated their chiefs; and of the causes which brought them into collision.

The English had made a first settlement on the Coromandel coast in the year 1625 at a small place, some thirty-six miles to the south of Madras, known now as Armagon. Seven years later they obtained from the Rájá of Bisnagar a small grant of land, called by the natives Chennapatanam from the village contained thereon. They re-named the place Madras, and built there a fort round their storehouses which they named Fort St. George. In 1653 the Company in London raised the agency at Madras to the position and rank of a Presidency. Towards the end of the seventeenth century the establishment there counted a population of 300,000 souls. In 1744 the town consisted of three divisions: that to the south (the White Town) extending about four hundred yards in length from north to south, and about one hundred yards in breadth. There resided the Europeans, mainly English. They had there about fifty houses, two churches, one of them Catholic; likewise the residence of the chief of the factory. All these were within the enclosure called Fort St. George. That somewhat pompous title represented merely a slender wall, defended by four bastions and as many batteries, very slight and defective in their construction, and with no outworks to defend them. This division was generally known as the 'White Town.' To the north of it, and contiguous, was another division, much larger and worse fortified, principally tenanted by Armenian and Indian merchants, called the Black Town. Beyond this, again to the north, was a suburb, where the poorer natives resided. These three divisions formed Madras. There were likewise to the south, about a mile distant from the White Town, two other large villages, inhabited solely by natives; but these were not included within that term. The English at this period did not exceedthree hundred in number, and of these two-thirds were soldiers, but few of whom had seen a shot fired.[2]

[2] Vide Orme's *History of Indostan* (Edition 1773), vol. i. p. 65.

The English colony in Madras was a trading colony. Not one of its members, up to this period, had the smallest thought of embroiling their presidency in the disputes which were frequent amongst the native chieftains. They wished to be let alone; to remain at peace; to conciliate friendship and goodwill. They were content to acknowledge the lords of the soil as their masters; to pay for the protection they enjoyed at their hands by a willing obedience; to ward off their anger by apologies and presents.

But there was a French colony also on the same coast, and in that a different policy had begun to prevail. In the year 1672 the King of Bijapur had sold to some French traders, led by a very remarkable man, Francis Martin, a tract of land on the Coromandel coast, eighty-six miles to the south-south-west of Madras. On this tract, close to the sea, was a little village called by the natives Puducheri. This the French settlers enlarged and beautified, and made their chief place of residence and trade. By degrees the name was corrupted to Pondicherry, a title under which it became famous, and under which it is still known.

So long as M. Martin lived, the policy of the French settlers was similar to that of the English at Madras. Nor did it immediately change when Martin died (December 30, 1706). Up to 1735, when M. Benoit Dumas was appointed Governor-General of the French possessions in India (for they had besides possessions on the Malabar coast and at Chandranagar, on the Húglí, in Bengal) it was in no way departed from. M. Dumas, however, almost immediately after his assumption of office, adopted the policy of allying himself closely with native princes; of taking part in their wars; with the view of reaping therefrom territorial and pecuniary advantage. This policy, of which he was the inventor, was, we shall see, carried to the most extreme length by his successor, M. Dupleix.

It will clear the ground for the reader if we add that the prosperity of the rival settlements was greatly affected by the action of their respective principals in Europe. On this point all the advantages lay with the English. For, whilst the Company of the Indies at Paris, and, it must be added, the French Government likewise, starved their dependency in India, and supplied them with inefficient and often ill-timed assistance, the East India Company, and the Government of the King of England, made a far better provision for the necessities of Madras.

It must, however, in candour be admitted that at the outset the French were better supplied with men and money than the English. Until the importance of the quarrel was recognized in Europe it became then a contest between the natural qualities of the men on the spot—a test of the capabilities of the races they represented.

I turn now, after this brief explanation of the position in Southern India in 1744, to describe the causes which led to the catastrophe which supervened very shortly after the arrival in India of the hero of this history.

CHAPTER III
HOW THE WAR IN THE KARNÁTIK AFFECTED THE FRENCH AND ENGLISH SETTLEMENTS

The trouble came from the Karnátik. The family of the chief who had held the position of Nawáb at the time of the death of Aurangzeb had adopted the new fashion, then becoming universal, of making the post hereditary in his family. Saádat-ullá Khán, the Nawáb in question, had himself been regularly appointed in 1710 by the court of Delhi. After a peaceful rule of twenty-two years he had died (1732) without issue, after having appointed his nephew, Dost Alí, to succeed him as Nawáb, the younger brother of Dost Alí, Bakar Alí, to be governor of the fort and district of Vellore; and Ghulám Husén, the nephew of his favourite wife, better known as Chánda Sáhib, to be Diwán, or prime minister, to his successor.

These dispositions were carried out. But they were by no means pleasing to the Súbahdár of the Deccan, the Nizám-ul-Múlk to whom the reader has been introduced. That eminent nobleman was not content that his subordinates should act as he was prepared to act himself. His sanction had not been obtained to the transaction. He used then his influence at Delhi to prevent the confirmation which, even in those disturbed times, every chieftain sought to obtain for every act of spoliation. For the moment he proceeded no further. He was content to leave Dost Alí in the position of a nobleman ruling without the authority of his liege lord, himself, or of the master of both, the court of Delhi.

Nizám-ul-Múlk had justly thought that time would avenge him. Four years after his accession, the death of the ruler of Trichinopoli induced Dost Alí to send an army under his son Safdar Alí and his Diwán Chánda Sáhib, to capture that fortress. Under the pretence of collecting revenue these two princes visited Madras and Pondicherry in their progress southwards, and at the latter place Chánda Sáhib entered into those intimate relations with the French which were to influence greatly the events which were to follow. They proceeded thence to Trichinopoli and took possession of the fortress, the widowed queen having, it is said, fallen in love with Chánda Sáhib. The latter remained there as governor, whilst Safdar Alí returned to his father at Arcot.

The new Diwán appointed in the place of Chánda Sáhib, Mír Ásad, began at once to insinuate charges of ambition against his predecessor, and expressed his opinion that Chánda Sáhib, once ruler of Trichinopoli, would not easily let go his hold. In this opinion he was supported by the Nawáb's eldest son, Safdar Jang. Doubtless they were right, but their utterances, freely expressed, served only to put Chánda Sáhib on his guard; and he commenced to store the fortress with provisions.

The acquisition of Trichinopoli by the Nawáb of the Karnátik had served only to inflame the mind of his liege lord, Nizám-ul-Múlk, against him. For a time, however, the disorders in Northern India, the threatened invasion of Nadír Sháh, and, finally, that invasion, held his hand. At last, however, his wrath over-mastered his judgement, and, in 1739, at the very time when the invasion of Nadír Sháh was in full swing, he gave permission to the Maráthás to attack Trichinopoli. In May of the following year, 1740, consequently, a Maráthá army of 10,000 men, led by Raghují Bhonsla, entered the Karnátik, met the hurriedly raised force of Dost Alí at the Damalcherri Pass, defeated it with great slaughter, and took prisoner the Diwán, Mír Ásad. Dost Alí was among the slain. The victors, then, listening to the persuasions of their prisoner, the Diwán, agreed to quit the province on receiving a payment, at stated intervals, of a total sum of ten million of rupees. Safdar Alí was then proclaimed Nawáb at Arcot, and Chánda Sáhib proceeded thither to do him homage.

During the preceding two years the French governor of Pondicherry, M. Dumas, had so strengthened the fortifications of that town, that it had come to be regarded by the natives as impregnable. During the Maráthá invasion, then, Chánda Sáhib had sent thither his family, and his example had been followed by Safdar Alí. After the installation of the latter at Arcot, the two princes proceeded to visit the French governor, who gave them a magnificent reception. On leaving, Safdar Alí took with him his family, whilst Chánda Sáhib, still suspecting danger, directed his own wives to remain at Pondicherry until events should more clearly develop themselves.

He had not to wait long. Safdar Alí, jealous of his prosperity, had induced the Maráthás, never unwilling, to make a fresh incursion into the Karnátik, and to dispose of Chánda Sáhib. In December of the same year then, just four years before Clive landed in India, those warriors entered the province, so deceived Chánda Sáhib as to induce him to sell them the ample stores of grain he had collected, and, as soon as they had received them, laid siege to Trichinopoli. Chánda Sáhib sustained a siege of nearly three months with great resolution, but then, his remaining stores of grain having been exhausted, was forced to surrender (March 26, 1741). The Maráthás, having plundered the town, departed for Sátára, taking with them Chánda Sáhib in close custody, and leaving one of their most famous leaders, of whom we shall hear further, Morári Ráo, with 14,000 of their best troops, to guard the place, and to act as discretion or greed might suggest.

The events I have recorded had encouraged among the nobles of the province a spirit of disorder in sympathy with the times. No man felt quite safe. Safdar Alí himself, but half reassured, sent for safety his family to the custody of the English at Madras, whilst, quitting the comparatively defenceless Arcot, he took up his abode in the strong fortress of Vellore. There his treasures had been stored, and there Murtizá Alí, who had married his sister, was governor. This man was treacherous, cowardly, and very ambitious. No sooner had he understood that his relationship by marriage did not shield him from the payment of money due to the Nawáb, than he proceeded to debauch the army, and to enlist on his side the neighbouring nobles. He then poisoned his brother-in-law. The poison not taking immediate effect, he persuaded a Patán to stab the Nawáb to the heart. He then declared himself Nawáb.

He was proclaimed alike at Vellore and Arcot. But his usurpation did not last long. Even in those days there was a public conscience, and the murder he had committed had been too brutal not to arouse indignation. The army rose against him. Fearing for his life, he disguised himself in woman's clothes, and escaped to Vellore.

On the flight of Murtizá Alí becoming known the army proclaimed Saiyud Muhammad Khán, the son of Safdar Alí, then residing at Madras under the protection of the English, to be Nawáb. The young prince and his mother were at once removed to the fort of Wandiwash, the ruler of which had married his father's sister.

It was this moment that Nizám-ul-Múlk chose as the time to intervene. Entering Arcot at the head of a large army (March, 1743) he completely pacified the province; then, marching on Trichinopoli, compelled the Maráthás to yield it and to evacuate the Karnátik. Possessing himself of the person of the newly proclaimed Nawáb, whom he declined to recognize, he proclaimed his own commander-in-chief, Khojá Abdullah, to be Nawáb of the Karnátik, and then returned to Golconda.

Unfortunately for the peace of the province Khojá Abdullah, a strong man, never took up the government of the Karnátik. He had returned with his master to Golconda, and had made there his preparations to set out. On the very morning which he had chosen for that purpose he was found dead in his bed. It was clear that he had been poisoned. Suspicion fell at once upon the nobleman who had originally been an urgent candidate for the office, and who now obtained it. He was an experienced soldier of good family, whose name was Anwar-ud-dín.

Nizám-ul-Múlk knew that the appointment would not be popular in the province so long as there should remain alive any member of the family of Saádat-ullá. He had therefore announced that the appointment of Anwar-ud-dín was provisional, and that the young prince, Saiyud Muhammad, already proclaimed Nawáb, should succeed to that post on his arriving at the age of manhood, remaining during the interval under the guardianship of Anwar-ud-dín, to be by him instructed in the art of governing. Anwar-ud-dín promised to carry out the will of his liege lord, and on his arrival in the Karnátik, assigned to the young prince the fort of Arcot, with a sufficient retinue of Patán soldiers. There the boy remained, treated with the deference due to his position.

But he was doomed. A few weeks after his arrival at Arcot it devolved upon him to preside at the wedding of one of his near relations. Amongst those who came to the ceremony was the murderer of his father, Murtizá Alí, laden with presents for the bridegroom. Strange as it may seem, the murderer was courteously received. But shortly after his entrance within the fort an unseemly disturbance was created by the disorderly entrance into the presence of thirteen Patán soldiers, who insolently demanded payment of the arrears they alleged to be due to them. With some difficulty they were forcibly ejected. But in the evening, as Anwar-ud-dín approached, attended by his courtiers and preceded by his guards, these thirteen Patáns managed to mingle with the latter, and one of them, rushing towards the daïs on which was the chair occupied by the young prince, ascended the steps leading to it, and, in a supplicatory attitude, made as though he would throw himself at his feet and demand pardon for the offence of the morning. But instead of this he plunged his dagger, which he had concealed on his person, into the prince's heart. He was almost instantly cut down by the attendants. The confusion was extreme. Suddenly it was discovered that Murtizá Alí had quitted the fort, had mounted his horse, and, accompanied by his armed followers, had galloped towards Vellore. Suspicion naturally fell upon this proved murderer, and the nobles generally endeavoured to exculpate themselves at his expense.

But suspicion fell likewise upon Anwar-ud-dín. Who, so much as he, would benefit by the death of Saiyud Muhammad? He was practically only guardian to the young prince, bound to resign his office as soon as the latter should attain his majority. Nor were these suspicions lessened when it was found that Nizám-ul-Múlk at once transmitted to Anwar-ud-dín a complete commission as Nawáb of Arcot. Vainly did the Nawáb deny all complicity in the bloody deed. Murtizá Alí was silent. 'It was supposed,' wrote Mr. Orme, 'that the only proofs he could have brought against Anwar-ud-dín would at the same time have condemned himself.' And this probably was true.

Such then was the political position in Southern India when Clive landed at Madras in 1744. The titular Emperor of Delhi was Muhammad Sháh, still reeling under the consequences of the invasion of Nadír Sháh and the sack of Delhi but five short years previously. The Súbahdár of the Deccan was still Nizám-ul-Múlk, possessing sufficient influence to have secured the succession in Southern India for his second son, Nasír Jang.[1] The Nawáb of the Karnátik, styled officially, of Arcot, was a stranger to the province, the unpopular and suspected Anwar-ud-dín. His authority there was not very secure. There were many pretenders waiting for the first mishap: amongst them his confederate in the murder of Saiyud Muhammad; Chánda Sáhib, still in confinement at Sátára; and many others. The elements of danger abounded everywhere. There were few petty chiefs who did not dub themselves 'Nawábs,' and aspire to positions higher than those held by them at the moment. The match alone was wanting to produce a general flame.

[1] Elliot's *History of India as told by its own Historians*, vol. viii. p. 113.

Under ordinary circumstances this state of affairs would not necessarily have affected the European settlers on the coast. But for them, too, the crisis was approaching. In 1740 the death of the Emperor, Charles VI, had thrown the greater part of Europe into a blaze. Three years later England had entered the field as an upholder of the Pragmatic Sanction. The news of this intervention, which necessitated war with France, reached India towards the close of 1744, and immediately affected the relations towards one another of the rival settlements on the Coromandel coast.

CHAPTER IV
HOW THE FORTUNES OF ROBERT CLIVE WERE AFFECTED BY THE HOSTILITIES BETWEEN THE FRENCH AND ENGLISH IN SOUTHERN INDIA

The events narrated in the second and third chapters must be studied by the reader who wishes to understand the India of 1744-65—the India which was to be the field for the exercise of the energies of the hero of this biography. It was an India, he will see, differing in all respects from the India of the present day: an India which may not improperly be termed an Alsatia, in which, as we have seen, murder was rampant, and every man fought for his own hand. What it then was it would be again were the English to leave the people to their own devices.

In the autumn of 1744 the Governor of Pondicherry, M. Dupleix, who had succeeded Dumas in October, 1741, received a despatch from his Directors notifying that a war with England was impending; requiring him to diminish his expenditure; to cease to continue to fortify Pondicherry; and to act with the greatest caution. A little later they wrote to say that war had actually been declared, that they had instructed the Governor of the Isle of France to proceed to the Indian Seas with a squadron he was preparing; and that they required him to second that officer, M. de la Bourdonnais, in his enterprise. Fearing, however, that La Bourdonnais might arrive off the coast only after some mischief had been done, they specially urged Dupleix to endeavour to arrange with the Governor of Madras that the war in Europe should not extend to the two settlements in India.

Similarly, the Governor of Madras, Mr. Morse, had received information and instructions from his masters. They were, however, of a nature differing in some respects from those received by the French authorities. They were to the effect that war had been declared; that he might at any moment expect the arrival of Commodore Barnett with a strong squadron off Madras, and that that squadron would be employed for the annihilation of the French commerce and the destruction of their possessions. It is easy to see, then, that when Morse received from the French Governor a proposal that the two settlements should preserve neutrality, he was compelled to decline it.

Thus threatened, for the reply of Mr. Morse led him to believe that the English would use their advantage to the utmost, Dupleix appealed to the common suzerain of the two settlements, to the Nawáb Anwar-ud-dín. He reminded him of the long-standing friendship between the rulers of the French settlement and his predecessors; how the French, in times of danger and difficulty, had ever extended their hospitality to the Nawábs and their friends; and represented in a striking manner the disadvantage which must accrue to the rulers of the Karnátik if the foreign settlements were to be permitted to wage war upon one another, for the reason that their respective nations had quarrelled in Europe. The mind of the Nawáb was much impressed by this cogent reasoning. He had no idea of the fighting qualities of the settlers. They had up to that time behaved as peaceful traders, deferential to the lords of the soil. He would that they should remain so. He therefore informed Mr. Morse that he would not permit an infraction of the peace between the two nations on the soil of the Karnátik.

For the moment the plague was stayed. Commodore Barnett's squadron arrived, intercepted and captured the French merchantmen, but could not attempt anything against Pondicherry. In April, 1746, Barnett died, and the command devolved upon Commodore Peyton. In June of the same year Peyton heard that some French vessels had been seen off Ceylon. They must be, he thought, the squadron of La Bourdonnais. He proceeded, then, to cruise off Negapatam to intercept it. On July 6, the two squadrons came in contact. They fought that afternoon and the next morning. After an indecisive combat on the 7th, the English commodore, finding that one of his best ships had sprung a leak, sheered off, and made sail for Trincomalee, leaving to the Frenchmen all the honours and advantage of the day. On the evening of the 8th of July the French squadron anchored off Pondicherry.

The result of the conference between the Admiral of the fleet and the Governor of Pondicherry was a resolution that the former should attack Madras, aided by the soldiers supplied by the latter. On the evening of the 12th of September, 1745, the French fleet sailed for Madras, arrived within cannon-shot of the English fort on the 15th at mid-day; La Bourdonnais then landed 1,100 European soldiers, some sipáhís, and a few Africans, and summoned the place to surrender.

Madras was in no position to resist him. The only chance possessed by Mr. Morse of saving the fort had lain in his obtaining from the Nawáb the protection which the latter had afforded to Pondicherry when he himself had threatened that town. He had applied for that protection, but in such a manner as to ensure the rejection of his prayer. He had sent his messenger empty-handed into the presence of Anwar-ud-dín, to demand as a right the protection which that nobleman had granted to Dupleix as a favour. The Nawáb, probably waiting for the presents which, as an Indian prince, he expected from the petitioner, had given no reply when the fleet of La Bourdonnais appeared before Madras on the 15th of September.

On the evening of the 19th the Governor sent a messenger to La Bourdonnais to treat. After much negotiation it was agreed that at noon of the day at which they had arrived, September 21, Fort St. George and the town of Madras should be surrendered to the French; that the English garrison and all the English in the town should become prisoners of war; that the civil functionaries should be set free on their parole that they should not carry arms against France until they should be regularly exchanged. There were other secret conditions, but it is unnecessary to the narrative to refer to these.[1]

[1] For a correct account of these see the author's *History of the French in India*, a new edition of which is about to appear.

The capture of Madras by the French took completely by surprise the Nawáb Anwar-ud-dín. On learning the movements of the French against that place he had despatched a special messenger ordering them to desist. The letter he conveyed reached Dupleix after Madras had been conquered, but whilst it remained still in the hands of La Bourdonnais. For a time he temporized with the Nawáb, whilst he endeavoured to bring La Bourdonnais, with whom he had difficulties as to the disposal of the place, to reason. A terrific storm heralding the north-east monsoon settled the second question by compelling the French admiral to sail for the islands with the remnant of the fleet it had scattered. On the 29th of October, Dupleix was sole director of French interests in India and on the Indian seas. His negotiations with the Nawáb were of a more complicated character. I lay particular stress upon them here because it was his action with reference to that potentate which inverted the position theretofore held between the native of India and the European; which called into the field the brilliant military qualities of Clive; which necessitated the long struggle for predominance in Southern India between France and England.

When day succeeded day and the Nawáb gradually came to the conviction that the audacious ruler of the French settlement had no real intention of transferring to him the conquest La Bourdonnais had made, he resolved to take it by force. He sent, therefore, his eldest son, Ma'afuz Khán, with a force of about 10,000 men, mostly cavalry, to enforce his demand. But, in face of the small French garrison occupying the place, these men soon discovered that they were powerless. When, with a great display of vigour, they had mastered the positions which secured a supply of water to the town, the garrison made a sortie and retook them. That was the first awakening. The second was more startling, more pregnant with consequences. A small force of 230 Europeans and 700 natives, sent by Dupleix under the command of a trusted officer named Paradis to relieve Madras, encountered the entire army of Ma'afuz Khán on the banks of the river Adyar, close to the village of Maliapur, then and to the present day known as St. Thomé,[2] defeated it with great slaughter, the Frenchmen wading breast-high through the water to attack the soldiers of the Nawáb. This victory, few in numbers as were the victors, must ever be regarded as pre-eminently a decisive battle. It brought into view, silently but surely, the possibility of the conquest of India by one or other of the two European powers on the Coromandel coast.

[2] From the fact identified by Bishop Heber and Professor H. H. Wilson, that it is the place where the Apostle St. Thomas is said to have been martyred on December 5, A.D. 58.

In a narrower sense it confirmed the possession of Madras to Dupleix. Thenceforth, as far as his eye could see, he had nought to fear in India. On the 9th of November Paradis entered Madras; he made there new provisions for the conquered English, confiscating all the merchandize that had been found within the town by La Bourdonnais. He then ordered all the English who should decline to take an oath of allegiance to the French governor within four days to quit the town; the English officials he permitted to dispose of their property; then to remove to Pondicherry as prisoners on parole. There were some amongst them who, possibly prescient of the future, declined to subscribe to terms which would tie their hands. These escaped to Fort St. David, a small fort purchased by the English in 1691, close to the important town of Gúdalúr, sixteen miles to the south of Pondicherry. Amongst these was the young writer who had had but two years' experience of India, and who was called Robert Clive.

Hardly had that young writer reached Fort St. David than he was called upon to share in its defence. It very soon became evident that the policy of Dupleix was a root-and-branch policy; that he was resolved to expel the English from all their settlements. With respect to Fort St. David, however, he was foiled partly by the stupidity of his generals, partly by the island stubbornness of the defenders. Four times did the French endeavour to take that small fort; four times, owing to circumstances upon which it is not necessary to enter, did they fail. Meanwhile there arrived an English squadron under Admiral Griffin, and later, to reinforce him, a fleet and army under Admiral Boscawen (August 11, 1748). By this arrival the positions of the rivals on the coast became inverted. From being besiegers the French became the besieged. For Boscawen at once laid siege to Pondicherry.

Then began (August 19, 1748) the first siege of Pondicherry by the English troops, assisted to a certain extent by those of the Nawáb. Many gallant deeds were performed on both sides. For a time Paradis was the soul of the defence. When he was killed, which happened whilst making a sortie on the 11th of September, the entire labour of directing the necessary measures fell upon Dupleix. In the attack were many good men and true. Boscawen himself gave an example of daring which was universally followed. Amongst those who were specially remarked was the hero of this book. A contemporary writer, whose journal[3] of the siege is before me, remarks regarding that young writer, that he 'served in the trenches on this occasion, and by his gallant conduct gave the first prognostic of that high military spirit, which was the spring of his future actions, and the principal source of the decisive intrepidity and elevation of mind, which were his characteristic endowments.' The efforts of the besiegers shattered, however, before the sturdy defence of the French. On the 17th of October the English were forced to raise the siege, leaving dead from the fire of the enemy or from sickness 1065 men. The English fleet remained for a year off the coast, and then sailed for England: the garrison, formerly the garrison of Madras and of Fort St. David, retired to the latter place, carrying with it Robert Clive, soon to be joined there by one of the most distinguished men whose careers have illustrated the history of the English in India, Major Stringer Lawrence.[4]

[3] See *Asiatic Annual Register* for 1802.

[4] Major Lawrence had arrived from England on the 13th of January 1747, commissioned to command all the Company's troops in India. From Mr. Forrest's Madras

Records we find that his salary as Major was £300 per annum, and 50 pagodas per month for other allowances, besides £70 per annum as third in Council. It was he who had repulsed the fourth attack made by the French on Fort St. David in the spring of that year. In the early days of the siege of Pondicherry he had had the misfortune to be taken prisoner. Released by the conditions of the treaty of Aix-la-Chapelle, he then resumed command at Fort St. David.

It is probable that, after the raising of the siege of Pondicherry, the French would have resumed their operations against Fort St. David, for, early in 1749, reinforcements in men and money had reached them. But before they could move, information reached them that, on the 7th of October, 1748, peace had been signed between the two nations at Aix-la-Chapelle. By the terms of this treaty the conquests made by the two countries were to be restored. The French, therefore, instead of renewing their attack on Fort St. David, were compelled to restore Madras, its fortifications undermined, and its storehouses empty.[5] This restoration was the more distasteful to them, when they found, as they very soon found, that from the force of events, the hostilities which had ceased in Europe were, by virtue of a legal fiction, to be continued in India. They were still to fight the battle for supremacy, not as principals, but as allies of the native princes who, in the disorder accompanying the catastrophe of the Mughal empire, fought for their own hand, against the native allies of the English.

[5] Forrest, page 4. The report which he gives *in extenso*, minuted by the Council of the Madras Presidency, runs as follows: 'The condition we have received it (Madras) in is indeed very indifferent, the French having undermined the fortifications, and rifled it of all useful and valuable stores.'

The official statement is quite opposed to the private accounts hitherto accepted as true.

CHAPTER V
CLIVE DECIDES FOR THE CAREER OF A SOLDIER

Before the conditions of the treaty of Aix-la-Chapelle had become known in India, the English governor of Fort St. David had despatched thence a small force of 430 Englishmen and 1000 sipáhís to assist the ex-Rájá of Tanjore, who had been dethroned for gross misconduct, to recover his kingdom. That, at least, was the nominal reason. The ambition to obtain for the English possession of Devikota, a fort on the river Coleroon, at the point where that river runs into the sea, was the true cause of the action. The force was commanded by Captain Cope, an officer of inferior merit. Clive accompanied it as a volunteer. The expedition failed from causes which it was impossible to combat. The ex-Rájá had no partisans, and the season was that of the monsoon-storms.

Still the idea was too popular to be abandoned. After the treaty between the two nations had reached India the expedition was therefore resumed. This time Major Lawrence, released by the action of that treaty, assumed the command. He took with him the entire available European force of the Company, leaving only a few to man the defences, and giving Clive a commission for the time only, to accompany him as lieutenant, proceeded to Devikota by sea, landed his troops, and commenced to batter the place. On the morning of the fourth day a practicable breach was pronounced, and a storming party was ordered. By his conduct Clive had already won the esteem of Lawrence,[1] and it was to him that he gave command of the party.

[1] The partiality which induced Lawrence to entrust Clive with so important a duty is to be found under his own hand. 'A man of undaunted resolution,' he writes in his memoirs, 'of a cool temper, and a presence of mind which never left him in the greatest danger. Born a

soldier, for, without a military education of any sort or much conversing with any of the profession, from his judgement and good sense, he led an army like an experienced officer and a brave soldier, with a prudence that certainly warranted success. This young man's early genius surprised and engaged my attention, as well before as at the siege of Devikota, where he behaved in courage and judgement much beyond what could have been expected from his years, and his success afterwards confirmed what I had said to so many people concerning him.' Cambridge's *War in India*, pp. 18-19.

To lead a storming party is an honour full of danger. So found Clive on this occasion. Of the twenty-nine Europeans who composed it, twenty-six were swept away by the enemy's horsemen, the sipáhís halting and witnessing the deed. Clive with the three survivors managed to join the main body which was advancing under Lawrence, and this body, repulsing a charge of cavalry which endeavoured to thwart it, pushed vigorously on, and stormed Devikota. Abandoning the cause of the ex-Rájá, Lawrence then made a treaty with the powers that were, in virtue of which Devikota was ceded to the East India Company, and the Rájá paid all the expenses of the war. The force returned to Fort St. David to find the fleet of Admiral Boscawen still off the coast.

But, during the absence of the English troops, there had occurred in the Karnátik one of those revolutions which were not uncommon in the days of the dissolution of the Mughal empire.

On the 17th of April, 1748, the titular King of Delhi, Muhammad Sháh, had died. His son, Ahmad Sháh, had succeeded him. Rather less than a month later, the Súbahdár of the Deccan, the famous Nizám-ul-Múlk, also died. He had in his lifetime arranged that the succession to the inheritance of the Deccan should devolve upon his second son, Nasír Jang, and Ahmad Sháh at once confirmed the nomination.[2] But those were not the days when a succession to vast power and great territories went unopposed. A claimant to the sovereignty of the Deccan soon appeared in the person of Muzaffar Jang, grandson of the late Súbahdár, and at the moment holding the government of Bíjapur. Not sufficiently powerful to press his claim without assistance Muzaffar Jang proceeded at once to Sátára, enlisted the Maráthás in his cause, persuaded them to release Chánda Sáhib, and to supply him with troops. The arrangement between the two princes was that, in case of success, Muzaffar Jang should become Súbahdár of the Deccan, Chánda Sáhib Nawáb of the Karnátik. It is necessary to state these facts clearly, because the war, thus initiated, formed the basis of the continued hostilities between the French and English after peace had been proclaimed in Europe.

[2] Elliott's *History of India*, pp. 112-3, vol. viii.

The reader may recollect that in the earlier part of this book[3] I have shown how Chánda Sáhib had formed a very high opinion of the French and how he had cultivated their friendship. Resolving now to avail himself of former favours, he made overtures to Dupleix, and obtained from him promise of substantial assistance. These promises were kept, and, towards the end of July, 1749, a detachment of French soldiers joined the armies of the two conspirators at the Damalcherri Pass. A few days later (August 3) they met at Ambúr the army of Anwar-ud-dín, completely defeated it, slew Anwar-ud-dín himself, took prisoner his eldest son, the Ma'afuz Khán who had been defeated by Paradis at St. Thomé, and forced the second son, Muhammad Alí, to save himself by flight to Trichinopoli. Marching straight to Arcot, Muzaffar Jang proclaimed himself Súbahdár of the Deccan, and Chánda Sáhib to be Nawáb of Arcot. As the French had espoused the cause of Chánda Sáhib it was natural that the English should sustain the claims of the rival. This rival was Muhammad Alí, the son of the late Nawáb, just escaped from the field of Ambúr. The two pretenders, whose cause had been adopted by the French, then proceeded to Pondicherry. There Dupleix, whose vision on political matters was remarkably clear, insisted that before committing themselves further, they should rid themselves of the only possible rival then at large, and should march against Trichinopoli. This they hesitated to do so long as the English fleet should remain off the coast.

[3] Chapter III.

This was the situation when Lawrence and Clive returned from the storming of Devikota. The chief of the English settlement was then Mr. Floyer, a gentleman who had a great dread of responsibility. The fighting party in the Council of Fort St. David urged that

Muhammad Alí should be supported, that the English fleet should remain off the coast, and that Trichinopoli should be defended. The admiral declared his willingness to remain if Mr. Floyer would only ask him. But Floyer shrank from the responsibility. Consequently the fleet sailed on the 1st of November, leaving behind 300 men as an addition to the garrison.

The very day after the disappearance of the English fleet had become known (November 2), Muzaffar Jang and Chánda Sáhib, with their French allies, marched towards Trichinopoli. But the two Indian princes had been most improvident. They had spent all their funds. To obtain more they assailed the strong fortress of Tanjore, captured one of the gates of the fortress, and forced the Rájá to agree to pay them very large sums. But the wily prince, learning that Nasír Jang was marching to his aid, managed to delay the chief payment until he had ascertained that the Súbahdár was within striking distance of the place. He then point-blank refused to hand over the money. The news of the approach of Nasír Jang spread disorder in the ranks of the armies of Muzaffar Jang and Chánda Sáhib, and they hurriedly retreated on Pondicherry.

Scenes of indescribable turmoil followed. In one of the skirmishes that ensued there occurred an event which, unpromising as it appeared at the outset, proved the means of the temporary accomplishment of the plans of the two conspirators. In a skirmish Muzaffar Jang was taken prisoner and placed in irons by the Súbahdár. When in that position, however, he managed to corrupt three of the principal chiefs who followed the banner of that prince. Their schemes were communicated to Chánda Sáhib and to his French allies. The result was that when the two rival armies joined battle at a place sixteen miles from the strong fortress of Gingi, which, meanwhile, the French under Bussy had captured, Nasír Jang's own levies turned against him and slew him; released Muzaffar Jang, and acknowledged him Súbahdár of the Deccan.

This event occurred on the 16th of December, 1750. Chánda Sáhib himself carried the news of the accomplished revolution from the battlefield to Pondicherry. The new Súbahdár followed him, and, for a while, French interests seemed predominant in the Karnátik. Then, for a moment, the tide seemed to ebb. On his way to Aurangábád Muzaffar Jang was slain by the very three conspirators who had compassed the death of his predecessor. The French troops with the force, commanded by the energetic Bussy, speedily avenged his death, and caused Salábat Jang, the third son of the late Nizám-ul-Múlk, to be proclaimed his successor. As Bussy with a force of French troops was to remain with him as his protector, it seemed as though French influence was destined to remain predominant in Southern India.

And so but for one man it would have remained, increasing its strength until its roots had spread far and wide below the surface. This, we believe, is the true lesson of the early part of this biography. It was one man's genius which, meeting the French on the ground of their own selection, seized their idea, made it his own, and worked it to their destruction. It was Clive who hoisted Dupleix with his own petard. We shall now see how.

After the return of the troops from the conquest of Devikota, the Government of Fort St. David had appointed Clive to be Commissary of the forces. Before, however, he could assume the duties of the office he had fallen sick, and had been sent by the doctors for a cruise in the Bay of Bengal. On his return thence in the early days of 1751 he found great demands on his activity. It devolved on him to equip a force of 280 English and 300 sipáhís, ordered, under Cope, to proceed to Trichinopoli, still threatened by the French and their allies. This accomplished, Clive was directed to accompany, as Commissary, a larger force of 500 English, 1000 sipáhís, and 100 Africans, ordered, under Captain Gingens, for Volkonda, 38 miles to the north-north-east of Trichinopoli, there to intercept a French force marching in that direction.

Gingens was not a strong officer, and by gross mismanagement he allowed the French to get the better of him. Clive, whose soldier's eye and martial instincts disapproved entirely of the evils he could not, from his position, prevent,[4] then and there quitted the force and returned to Fort St. David.

[4] Captain Dalton, who served under Captain Gingens, writes of him in his journal as 'a man of unfortunately jealous temper which made him mistrust the goodwill of any who offered to give him advice.' Vide *Memoir of Captain Dalton*, 1886, pp. 93-4.

The return of Clive was opportune. The new Governor, Mr. Saunders, a man of a large and comprehensive intellect, was waiting the arrival of troops from England to fit out a new expedition of 80 Englishmen and 300 sipáhís to convoy provisions to Trichinopoli. He had no officer, however, to whom he dared entrust the command. A civilian of his Council, Mr. Pigot, was then deputed to lead the force the first forty miles, when it would be beyond the reach of hostile attack, and Clive volunteered to go with him. The force set out in July, 1751, and on the third day reached Verdachelam, the point indicated. Thence the two English civilians turned back as had been arranged, and, though attacked on the way by a swarm of native horsemen, reached Fort St. David in safety. The detachment then marched through a safe country to Trichinopoli.

A few days later fresh troops arrived from England. Mr. Saunders was anxious to despatch these to reinforce the troops under Gingens, but again the same difficulty presented itself. Meanwhile Clive had deliberately considered his position. As a civilian, he had had a career which did not satisfy him. As Commissary, it had been his fate to witness the inefficient leading of others, without any authority to interfere. He felt within him the power to command. His transfer to the military service would, he saw, relieve the Governing Council from a great difficulty, and give him, possibly, a command which he could exercise for the benefit of his country. Very soon did he decide. Mr. Saunders, whose appreciation of him was not inferior to that of Major Lawrence, sanctioned the transfer of his name to the military list, bestowed upon him the commission of captain,[5] and directed him to proceed at once, with a detachment of the few troops available, to Devikota, to place himself there under the orders of Captain Clarke, whose total force would thus be augmented to 100 English, 50 sipáhís, and one field-piece. The two officers were then to march with this detachment to Trichinopoli. There Clive was to take stock of the position and report to Mr. Saunders.

[5] The order of appointing Clive ran as follows:—'Mr. Robert Clive, who has lately been very serviceable in conducting several parties to camp, offering to go, without any consideration of pay, provided we will give him a Brevet to entitle him to the rank of a Captain, as he was an Officer at the Siege of Pondichery, and almost the whole time of the War, and distinguished himself on many occasions, it is conceived that this Officer may be of some service, and, therefore, now ordered that a Brevet be drawn out, and given him.' Forrest.

This happened towards the end of July, 1751.

CHAPTER VI
THE FIRST YEAR OF SOLDIERING AT TRICHINOPOLI AND ARCOT

The state of affairs in Trichinopoli was sufficient to cause considerable alarm as to the result of the war. Chánda Sáhib was besieging that fortress with a very large native force, aided by 900 Frenchmen. His rival, Muhammad Alí, depended solely on the 600 English who were assisting him, for of his own troops there were but 5000, and of these 2000 were horsemen.

But that which most impressed Clive when he arrived there with Captain Clarke early in August was the depression which filled the minds of the native prince and the English soldiers. The treasury of Muhammad Alí was exhausted, and he despaired of success. The English soldiers had no confidence in their leaders, and, with a few exceptions,[1] the leaders had no confidence in themselves. To rouse leaders and men from their apathy Clive felt that something startling must be attempted. Not indeed at Trichinopoli, for Captain Gingens, who commanded there, though a brave man, was scarcely equal to taking a bold initiative in face of the preponderating troops of the enemy. Alike at school, and in his researches in the

Governor's library at Madras, Clive had read of the achievements of great commanders who, pressed hard by enemies at home, had changed the fate of the campaign by carrying the war into the enemy's country. What an opportunity for such a strategy where he was! To take Trichinopoli Chánda Sáhib had massed all, or nearly all, his available troops before that place, leaving the capital of the Karnátik, Arcot, absolutely denuded of trustworthy fighting men. The true method of relieving the former place was to seize and hold the latter. Impressed with this idea, Clive returned to Fort St. David and communicated it to Mr. Saunders. This large-minded man embraced the plan with fervour, and although at the two principal places held by the English, Madras and Fort St. David, he had but 350 English soldiers, he resolved to risk 200 of them on the expedition.[2] The command of it he gave to Clive, but one month before a simple civilian, and despatched him forthwith to Madras, to march thence with his raw levies, most of them recently arrived from England.

[1] One of these exceptions was Captain John Dalton, whose journal, published in 1886 (Messrs. W. H. Allen & Co.), adds much to our knowledge of the individuals engaged in the campaign.

[2] Forrest, page 10. The Board unanimously concurred with Mr. Saunders.

It was on the 26th of August, 1751, that Clive set forth from Madras on the march which was to bring to him immortal fame, and to secure for his countrymen the first footing on the ladder which was to conduct them to empire. He had with him 200 English soldiers, 300 sipáhís, and three small field-pieces. Of his eight officers, four were volunteers from the civil service who, with two of the others, had never been under fire. On the 29th the little force reached Kanchípuram, 42 miles from Madras and 27 from Arcot. There he learned that that place was garrisoned by about 1200 native soldiers, that the discipline was lax, and that a surprise was quite feasible; but that the place itself was capable of a good defence. He did not wait longer. Setting out in a terrible storm, he reached the vicinity of Arcot on the 31st, surprised the fort, and compelled the town to surrender, without losing a single man. Having taken measures to store provisions, he marched on the 4th September to the mud fort of Tímerí, frightened the 600 native soldiers encamped there into retreating, and returned. Two days later, having been informed that the enemy had again gathered there to the number of 2000, he marched again against them, attacked and completely defeated them. From want of heavy guns he did not take the fort.

Relieved from the chances of immediate attack, Clive returned to improve, as far as he could, the defences of the place he had captured. One of his first acts had been to write to Madras for some 18-pounder guns. These were at once despatched. But the enemy, now fully awake, attempted to intercept them at Kanchípuram. To save his guns Clive marched thither with all his force except 80 men. He did save the guns, but the enemy, profiting by his absence, attacked Arcot with all their available numbers. The garrison, however, small as it was (30 Englishmen and 50 sipáhís), had become imbued with their leader's spirit. They repulsed the attack, Clive brought the guns into the fort, and the enemy dispersed.

Meanwhile the news of the brilliant enterprise had spread far and wide; had brought hope to the defenders of Trichinopoli, and alarm and irritation to Chánda Sáhib and his French allies. More even than that. The important kingdom of Mysore, the ruler of which had been long pressed by the rival combatants, declared now in favour of Muhammad Alí, and sent an army under its Dalwai (Prime Minister) to assist him. The native chiefs who ruled the territories which connected the beleaguered town with the eastern coast followed the example of Mysore;—an enormous gain, for it ensured the safety of the English convoys from the coast. Greatly impressed with these defections, Chánda Sáhib at once despatched 3000 of his best troops to join the forces which his son, Rájá Sáhib, was commanding in North Arcot. There they would be joined by 150 Frenchmen. One of Clive's objects had thus been already attained. The capture of Arcot had enormously weakened the enemy's attack: had more than proportionately increased the strength of the defence of Trichinopoli.

The eyes of India south of the great Vindhyan range were now turned upon Arcot. Upon its successful or unsuccessful defence depended the future in India of the two European nations which, though nominally at peace, were warring desperately against each other. The siege began on the 23rd of September. It was characterized by extraordinary tenacity, great daring, infinite powers of resource, on the part of Clive and the defenders.

The sipáhís vied with the English alike in courage and in capacity to withstand fatigue, hunger, and thirst. Their self-denial, displayed when they insisted that the water which was brought to them under much difficulty should be offered first to their European comrades, went the round of the world. It gave evidence of the cordiality which was to exist for a century, and to be renewed in 1861-2 under conditions more favourable than ever. At length, after more than seven weeks of continuous pounding, the breach became practicable. The rumour that the great Maráthá soldier, Morári Ráo, was approaching the place to lend a hand to Clive, determined Rájá Sáhib to utilize his advantage without delay. On the 14th of November he sent every available man to the breach. The garrison, enfeebled though they were by privations, few in number from their losses, separated by the necessities of the defence, met their assailants with a courage as stern, a resolution as dogged, as that which, in difficult circumstances, English soldiers have always displayed. After an hour's fierce fighting, in which the French took no part, the besiegers fell back, beaten, baffled, and humiliated. At two o'clock that afternoon they begged to be allowed to bury their dead. At two o'clock the following morning they disappeared in the direction of Vellore.

Thus ended the siege of Arcot. It had lasted fifty days. The manner in which it ended gave the English, and especially the English leader, a prestige which had an enormous effect on the campaigns that followed. What a great thing this much-abused 'prestige' is in India was illustrated by the fact that the minds of the native princes and peoples all over the southern part of the peninsula turned to Clive as to a master whom they would follow to the death. He inverted the positions of the two nations, confounded by his brilliant action the schemes of Dupleix, and, very soon afterwards, was able to impose his will, representing the will of the English nation, upon all the native princes who ruled or reigned in the territories of Haidarábád and the Karnátik.

For—another great feature in the character of this man—Clive never left a work half-finished. The blow, he felt, was weak and paltry unless it were driven home. So he felt, so he acted, on this occasion. On the 19th he took Timerí, the fort which had before baffled him. Joined then by Morári Ráo with 1000 Maráthá horsemen, he marched on Arni, seventeen miles south of Arcot, to attack Rájá Sáhib, who had taken post there with the army which had lately besieged him, reinforced by French troops just arrived from Pondicherry. The superiority in numbers of the force of Rájá Sáhib was so great that, when he noted the approach of Clive, he turned to meet him. Clive halted where he was. He had recognized that his position was excellent for defence, covered in front by rice-fields impracticable for guns, on the right by a village, and on the left by a grove of palm-trees. There he ranged his troops to meet the threatened attack.

It came very quickly, for the space between the two forces was but 300 yards. The enemy had discovered a narrow causeway leading across the marshy ground to the village on Clive's right. Heralding their approach with an advance of cavalry, they directed a portion of their horsemen to assail the village on the right; another portion to drive Morári Ráo from the grove; whilst the main body of the infantry should cross the causeway. The last-named was a dangerous operation in the face of a man like Clive, for whilst the narrowness of the causeway rendered the advance slow, it gave time to Clive to concentrate upon it the fire of his guns. And this he did. For a time the French, who led the attack, marched boldly. At length they came under the full fire of the guns. It was the story of the bridge of Arcola, but there was no Bonaparte to lead them on. They hesitated, halted, then fell back with precipitation; and, quitting the causeway, formed on the rice-fields, almost touching the cavalry on their left, who were fighting fiercely to gain an entrance into the village. This was the supreme moment, and Clive's genius utilized it to the utmost. Whilst the enemy were busily engaged on the right and left, their centre still reeling under the losses sustained on the causeway, he detached a body of English soldiers into the village, directing them to seize the head of the causeway, and, traversing it rapidly with a portion of the sipáhís, to dash on the enemy's centre, and seize their guns. Well was he served. No sooner did the enemy perceive the English on the causeway than a panic struck their centre, and they hastened to fall back. The panic communicated itself to the two wings, already severely handled; they too let go their hold, and turned to follow their comrades. True to the principle referred to in a preceding page, Clive pressed them hardly, not staying pursuit until darkness rendered it fruitless. The record of this, his first real battle, fought against more than double his numbers, was a splendid one. Whilst his own losses were but eight sipáhís of his own force, and some fifty horsemen of his Marátha allies, there were killed or wounded fifty Frenchmen and about three times that number of the natives. Whilst the English had fought mostly under cover, the enemy had had the disadvantage of being exposed, especially on the causeway.

Fit sequel to the defence of Arcot was this fight at Arni. It dispersed the army of Rájá Sáhib, caused many of his soldiers, always in the East inclined to side with the strongest, to desert to the victors; it induced the ruler of the fort of Arni to declare for Muhammad Alí; and it deprived the enemy of their military chest. From its field Clive marched rapidly on Kanchípuram, took possession, after a short siege, of the strong pagoda which, meanwhile, had been seized by the enemy; then, having placed in Arcot a sufficient garrison, returned to Madras, thence to Fort St. David, having carried out to the letter the programme he had submitted at the latter place to Governor Saunders.

Well had he done it. The army of Chánda Sáhib, doubled up by the terrible blow struck in the very centre of his possessions, still indeed held the position before Trichinopoli, but, from an enemy confident, boastful, certain of ultimate success, he had become an enemy timid, irresolute, doubtful of the issue, shrinking from his own shadow. The prestige gained by the young Englishman paralyzed his vitality. It required apparently but one more blow to complete his demoralization. The one condition of that blow was that it must be struck quickly, suddenly, before the enemy should have time to recover. Considerations such as these, we may be sure, formed the staple of the conversations at Fort St. David between the young captain and the Governor after the return of the former from Arcot.

CHAPTER VII
"THE SWELL AND DASH OF A MIGHTY WAVE"[1]

[1] 'The battle of Napoleon was the swell and dash of a mighty wave before which the barrier yielded, and the roaring flood poured onwards, covering all things.' Sir W. Napier's *Peninsular War*.

But there was one distinguished actor in the events I have recorded who was by no means inclined to sit passively under the severe blow which had but just upset all his calculations. This man was Dupleix, the Governor of Pondicherry. The plan of taking Trichinopoli had been his plan. To take that place he had used all the resources open to him: he had, in fact, for that purpose pawned the resources of Pondicherry. But one thing he had not done. He had not removed from the court of the Súbahdár the one competent general, Bussy-Castelnau, generally known as Bussy, to carry out his ideas. He had bent all his hopes on Law of Lauriston, nephew of the famous Scotch financier, and who commanded the French troops before Trichinopoli. He leant, however, on a reed, on which, when a man leaneth, it pierces his hand. As a soldier under command Law was excellent. As a Commander-in-chief he was pitiable, dreading responsibility, timid, nervous, wanting in every quality of a general. At the moment Dupleix did not know this. He had seen Law fight well and gallantly at the siege of Pondicherry: he had known him full of self-confidence, and he had believed him capable of great things.

When, then, Clive struck that blow at the middlepiece of the Karnátik dominion, which paralyzed the army before Trichinopoli, Dupleix, whose brain had not been paralyzed, sent the most pressing orders to Law not to care for events passing at Arcot, but to redouble his efforts against the fortress he was besieging, to use every effort to take the place before

Clive's unexpected blow should produce its natural consequences. To accomplish this end he despatched to him a battering-train and all the Frenchmen he had available.

Dupleix could transmit his orders, but he could not send with them the daring spirit which inspired them. Law had before Trichinopoli 900 French soldiers, of excellent quality, 2000 sipáhís trained in the French fashion, and the army of Chánda Sáhib. It was a force to attempt anything with in India. If a superior officer on the spot had said to Law 'Attack!' he would have attacked with conspicuous courage. But it was the weakness of his nature that, being in command, he could not say the word himself. Therefore he did nothing.

But to Clive, recognizing all that was possible, ignorant only of the character of the French commander, the situation seemed full of danger. He must strike again, and strike immediately. The successful blow at the middlepiece must be followed up by a blow at the head. That head was Trichinopoli. He prepared therefore, as soon as the recruits expected from England should arrive, to march to that place, and compel the raising of the siege.

Dupleix had divined all this. Once again was this young Englishman to baffle him. As Law would not act he must devise some other means to defeat him. Why, he said to himself, should I not take a leaf from the Englishman's book, reconquer Arcot, possibly attack Madras, and make it evident to the native princes that Pondicherry is still the stronger? The idea pleased him, and he proceeded, in the most secret manner, to act upon it.

Incited by the urgent requests and promises of Dupleix, Rájá Sáhib, the beaten of Arni, quietly levied troops, and joined by a body of 400 Frenchmen, appeared suddenly before Punamallu on the 17th of January. Punamallu is a town and fort in the Chengalpat district, thirteen miles west-south-west from Madras. The town, but not the fort, fell at once into the hands of the enemy. Had the allies then marched on Madras they might have taken it, for it had but a garrison of 100 men. They preferred, however, to march on Kanchípuram. There they repaired the damages the English had done to the defences of the great pagoda, and, leaving 300 sipáhís to defend it, marched to Vendalúr, twenty-five miles to the south of Madras, and established there a fortified camp, whence they levied contributions on the surrounding country. Their plan was so to coerce northern Arcot as to compel the English to quit Trichinopoli, to save it.

They had succeeded in thoroughly alarming alike the English and the petty chieftains in alliance with them when information of their action reached Fort St. David. There Clive and Saunders were busily engaged in preparing for the new expedition which the former was to lead, as soon as the drafts from England should arrive, to the relief of Trichinopoli. The information changed all their plans. Saunders at once sent a pressing message to Bengal to despatch all available English soldiers to Madras. Thither Clive proceeded; took command of the 100 Englishmen forming its garrison; and ordered from Arcot four-fifths of the troops stationed there. On the 20th of February the troops from Bengal arrived: on the 21st the Arcot garrison was within a march of Madras. On the following morning Clive quitted that fort, and, joined as he marched forth by the men from Arcot, took the direction of Vendalúr, having, all told, 380 Englishmen, 1300 sipáhís, and six field-pieces. His movements, however, had become known to the enemy. These, therefore, had quitted Vendalúr on the night of the 21st; had marched by various routes to Kanchípuram; and, re-uniting there, had pushed with all speed towards Arcot. There they had made arrangements to be received, but their plot had been discovered, and finding their signals unanswered, they had marched to Káveripák, a town ten miles to the east of Arcot. There, in front of the town, they encamped, in a position previously carefully chosen as the one most likely to invite surprise, for which they proceeded to thoroughly prepare themselves.

Clive, meanwhile, had been marching on Vendalúr. He had made some way thither when scouts reached him with the news that the birds had flown, and in different directions. To gain further information he continued his march and reached Vendalúr. After staying there five hours certain information reached him that he would find the enemy at Kanchípuram. Thither he proceeded, and there he arrived at four o'clock on the morning of the 23rd, having made a forced march, with a rest of five hours, of forty-five miles. It was then nine o'clock in the morning, and he resolved to rest for the day.

But, after his men had slept a few hours, the anxiety of Clive regarding Arcot impelled him to break their slumbers, and order them forward. They set out accordingly about one o'clock, and about sunset came in sight of Káveripák, but not of the French hidden in front of it. The French leader, in fact, had laid his plans with the greatest skill. A thick mango-grove, covered along two sides by a ditch and bank, forming almost a redoubt, roughly fortified along the faces by which the English must advance, covered the ground about 250 yards to the left of the road looking eastwards. There the French had placed, concealed from view, their battery of nine guns and a portion of their best men. About a hundred yards to the right of the road, also looking eastwards, was a dry watercourse, along the bed of which troops could march, sheltered, to a great extent, from hostile fire. In this were massed the rest of the infantry, native and European. The cavalry was in the rear, hidden by the grove, ready to be launched on the enemy when they should reach the ground between the watercourse and the grove. The men were on the alert, expecting Clive.

The space at my disposal will not permit me to give the details of the remarkable battle[2] which followed. It must suffice to say that no battle that was ever fought brought into greater prominence the character of its commander. In the fight before Káveripák we see Clive at his best. He had marched straight into the trap, and, humanly speaking, was lost. It was his cool courage, his calmness in danger, his clearness of mind in circumstances of extraordinary difficulty, his wonderful accuracy of vision, the power he possessed of taking in every point of a position, and of at once utilizing his knowledge, that saved him. He was, I repeat, lost. He had entered the trap, and its doors were fast closing upon him. Bravely did his men fight to extricate him from the danger. Their efforts were unavailing. Soon it came about that the necessity to retreat entered almost every mind but his own. Even the great historian of the period, Mr. Orme, wrote that 'prudence counselled retreat.' But to the word prudence Clive applied a different meaning. To him prudence was boldness. What was to become of the British prestige, of the British position in Southern India, if he, without cavalry, were to abandon the field to an enemy largely provided with that arm, and who would be urged to extraordinary energy by the fact that the unconquered hero of Arcot had fled before them?

[2] The reader who would care to read such a detailed account will find it in the writer's *Decisive Battles of India*, ch. ii.

No: he would think only of conquering; and he conquered. After four hours of fighting, all to his disadvantage, he resolved to act, *in petto*, on the principle he had put into action when he first seized Arcot. He would carry the war into the enemy's position. By a very daring experiment he discovered that the rear of the wooded redoubt occupied by the French had been left unguarded. With what men were available he stormed it; took the enemy by surprise, the darkness wonderfully helping him; and threw them into a panic. Of this panic he promptly took advantage; forced the Frenchmen to surrender; then occupied their strong position, and halted, waiting for the day. With the early morn he pushed on and occupied Káveripák. The enemy had disappeared. The corpses of fifty Frenchmen and the bodies of 300 wounded showed how fierce had been the fight. He had, too, many prisoners. His own losses were heavy: forty English and thirty sipáhís. But he had saved Southern India. He had completely baffled the cunningly devised scheme of Dupleix.

The consequences of the battle were immediately apparent. Northern Arcot having been freed from enemies, Clive returned to Fort St. David, reached that place the 11th of March, halted there for three days, and was about to march to strike a blow at the other extremity, Trichinopoli, when there arrived from England his old and venerated chief, Stringer Lawrence. The latter naturally took command, and two days later the force Clive had raised, and of which he was now second in command, started with a convoy for Trichinopoli. On the 26th it was met eighteen miles from that fortress by an officer sent thence to inform Lawrence that the French had despatched a force to intercept him at Koiládí, close to and commanding his line of advance. By great daring, Lawrence made his way until he had passed beyond the reach of the guns of the badly-commanded enemy and the fort, and before daybreak of the following morning was joined by a small detachment of the garrison: another, of greater force, met him a little later. He had, in fact, practically effected a junction with the beleaguered force at the outpost of Elmiseram when he learned that the French were marching against him. They contented themselves, however, with a fierce cannonade: for, as Clive advanced to cover the movement of the rest of the force, they drew back, and Lawrence, with his troops, and the convoy he was escorting, entered Trichinopoli. The French commander was so impressed by this feat of arms, which gave the defenders, now assisted by Morári Ráo and the Dalwai of Mysore, a strength quite equal to his own, that he fell back into the island of Seringham. There he was faced on one side by Lawrence. To cut off his communications with the country on the further side of the river Kolrun, Lawrence despatched Clive[3] with 400 English and some 700 sipáhís, accompanied by some Marátha and Tanjore cavalry, to occupy the village of Samiáveram, a village commanding with three others the exit from the island on the only practicable route. Clive set out on the 7th of April, occupied Samiáveram the same day, and, two days later, made his position stronger by storming and occupying the pagoda of Mansurpet, and the mud fort of Lalgudi. There still remained Paichanda. The occupation of this would complete the investment of the island on that side.

[3] It is a striking testimony to the prestige Clive had already acquired with the native princes that when Muhammad Alí, the Dalwai, and Morári Ráo were consulted by Lawrence as to co-operating in the expedition, they consented only on the condition that Clive should command.

Meanwhile Dupleix, thoroughly disgusted with Law had despatched M. d'Auteuil with a small force to take command in his place. Whilst Clive was engaged in occupying the two places he had stormed, and was preparing to attack the third, d'Auteuil was approaching the town of Utátur, fifteen miles beyond Samiáveram, the headquarters of Clive. He arrived there on the 13th of April, and although his force—120 Frenchmen, 500 sipáhís, and four field-pieces—was far inferior to that of Clive, he resolved to make a flank-march to the river and open communications with Law. He sent messengers to warn that officer of his intention, and to beg him to despatch troops to meet him. But Clive captured one of these messengers, and resolved to foil his plans.

D'Auteuil had set out on the morning of the 14th, but had not proceeded far when he noticed the English force barring the way, and returned promptly to Utátur. Clive then fell back on Samiáveram.

There was a strongly fortified pagoda, named Paichanda, on the north bank of the Kolrun, forming the principal gateway into the island of Seringham, which Clive had intended to take, but which, owing to the movements of d'Auteuil, he had not yet attempted. On receiving the message from d'Auteuil of which I have spoken, Law had resolved to debouch by this gateway, and fall on Clive whilst he should be engaged with d'Auteuil. But, when the time for action came, unable to brace himself to an effort which might have succeeded, but which possessed some element of danger, he despatched only eighty Europeans, of whom one-half were English deserters, and 700 sipáhís, to march by the portal named, advance in the dark of the night to Samiáveram, and seize that place whilst Clive should be occupied elsewhere. The knowledge of English possessed by the deserters would, he thought, greatly facilitate the task.

His plan very nearly succeeded to an extent he had never contemplated. Clive had returned from his demonstration against d'Auteuil, and, worn out and weary, had laid himself down to sleep in a caravanserai behind the smaller of the two pagodas occupied as barracks by his men. They also slept. This was the position within the village when a spy, sent forward by the leader of the surprising party, returned with the information that Clive and his men were there, and were sleeping. This news decided the commander to press on and to seize the great Englishman where he lay. By means of his deserters he deceived the sentries. One of the former, an Irishman, informed the tired watchmen that he had been sent by Lawrence to strengthen Clive. The party was admitted, and one of the garrison was directed to lead its members to their quarters. They marched quietly through the lines of sleeping Maráthás and sipáhís till they reached the lesser pagoda. There they were again challenged. Their reply was a volley through its open doors on the prostrate forms within it. They went on then to the caravanserai and repeated their action there.

Again was Clive surprised. Once more were the coolness, the clearness of intellect, the self-reliance, of one man pitted against the craft and wiles of his enemies. Once again did the one man triumph. He was, I repeat, as much surprised as the least of his followers. Let the reader picture to himself the situation. To wake up in darkness and find an enemy, whose numbers were unknown, practically in possession of the centre of the town, in the native inn of which he had gone peacefully to sleep but two hours before; his followers being shot down; some of them scared; all just awakening; none of them cognizant of the cause of the uproar; many of the intruders of the same nation, speaking the same language as himself; all this occurring in the sandy plains of India: surely such a situation was sufficient to test the greatest, the most self-reliant, of warriors. It did not scare Clive. In one second his faculties were as clear as they had ever been in the peaceful council chamber. He recognized, on the instant, that the attackers had missed their mark. They had indeed fired a volley into the caravanserai in which he had lain with his officers, and had shattered the box which lay at his feet and killed the sentry beside him, but they had not stopped to finish their work. Instantly Clive ran into one of the pagodas, ordered the men there, some two hundred, to follow him, and formed them alongside of a large body of sipáhís who were firing volleys in every direction, whom he believed to be his own men. To them he went, upbraided them for their purposeless firing, and ordered them to cease. But the men were not his men, but French sipáhís. Before he had recognized the fact, one of them made a cut at him with his talwar, and wounded him. Still thinking they were his own men, Clive again urged them to cease fire. At the moment there came up six Frenchmen, who summoned him to surrender. Instantly he recognized the situation. Instantly his clear brain asserted itself. Drawing himself up he told the Frenchmen that it was for them and not for him to talk of surrender; bade them look round and they would see how they were surrounded. The men, scared by his bearing, ran off to communicate the information to their commander. Clive then proceeded to the other pagoda to rally the men posted there. The French sipáhís took advantage of his absence to evacuate the town. The Frenchmen and the European deserters meanwhile had occupied the lesser pagoda. They had become by this time more scared than the surprised English. Their leader had recognized that he was in a trap. His mental resources brought to him no consolation in his trouble. He waited quietly till the day broke, and then led his men into the open. But Clive had waited too; and when the Frenchmen emerged, he received them with a volley which shot down twelve of them. They hurried back to their place of shelter, when Clive, wishing to stop the effusion of blood, me to the front, pointed out to them their hopeless position, and offered them terms. One of them, an Irishman, levelled his musket at Clive, and fired point-blank at him. The ball missed Clive, but traversed the bodies of two sergeants behind him. The French commander showed his disapproval of the act by surrendering with his whole force. Clive had sent the Maráthás and the cavalry to pursue the French sipáhís. These caught them, and cut them up, it is said, to a man.

Thus ended the affair at Samiáveram. I have been particular in giving the details which illustrate the action of Clive, because they bring home to the reader the man as he was: a man not to be daunted, clear and cool-headed under the greatest difficulties; a born leader; resolute in action; merciful as soon as the difficulties had been overcome: a man, as Carlyle wrote of another, not less distinguished in his way, 'who will glare fiercely on an object, and see through it, and conquer it; for he has intellect, he has will, force beyond other men.'

The end was now approaching. On the 15th of May, Clive captured Paichanda. He then marched on Utátur, forced d'Auteuil to retreat on Volkonda, and, following him thither, compelled him (May 29) to surrender. Three days later Law followed his example. The entire French force before Trichinopoli gave itself up to Major Lawrence. Its native allies did the same. The one regrettable circumstance in the transaction was the murder of Chánda Sáhib at the instance of his rival.

After this, Clive returned to Fort St. David; was employed during the fall of the year in reducing places which still held out against the Nawáb. This campaign tried his constitution, already somewhat impaired, very severely, and on its conclusion, in the beginning of October, he proceeded to Madras to rest from his labours. There he married Miss Maskeleyne, the sister of a fellow-writer, with whom, in the earlier days of his Indian life, he had contracted a friendship. But his health continued to deteriorate, and he was forced to apply for leave to visit Europe. This having been granted, he quitted Madras in February, 1753, full of glory. His character had created his career. But for his daring, his prescience, his genius, and his great qualities as a soldier, it is more than probable that

Dupleix would have succeeded in establishing the basis of a French empire in Southern India.

CHAPTER VIII
CLIVE IN ENGLAND; AND IN BENGAL

The visit of Clive to England was scarcely the success hoped for. His fame had preceded him, and the Court of Directors had assured him, through the Governor of Madras, that they had 'a just sense of his services.' Perhaps the person who had been the most astonished at his brilliant success was his own father. He had remarked, when he first heard of his victories, that 'the booby had some sense after all.' But then it must be recollected that the father had seen but little of the boy during his childhood and growing years, and that his unfavourable impression had been derived probably from the aversion shown by the lad to enter his own profession. But even he, now, was prepared to follow the stream, and give a hearty reception to the defender of Arcot. So, at first, Clive was fêted and toasted in a manner which must have convinced him that his services were appreciated. The Court of Directors carried out the promise I have referred to by giving a great banquet in his honour, and by voting him a diamond-hilted sword as a token of their esteem. This honour, however, Clive declined unless a similar decoration were also bestowed upon the chief under whom he had first served, Major Stringer Lawrence.

Clive had earned sufficient money to live with great comfort in England. He did not look forward then to return to India as an absolute certainty. Rather he desired to enter Parliament, and await his opportunity. It happened that the year following his arrival the dissolution of the existing Parliament gave him an opportunity of contesting the borough of St. Michael in Cornwall. He was returned as a supporter of Mr. Fox, but the return was petitioned against, and although the Committee reported in his favour, the House decided, from a purely party motive, to unseat him. This disappointment decided Clive. He had spent much money, and with this one result—to be thwarted in his ambition. He resolved then to return to the seat of his early triumphs, and applied to the Court for permission to that effect.

The Court not only granted his request, but obtained for him the commission of lieutenant-colonel in the royal army, and named him Governor and Commander of Fort St. David, with succession to the Governorship of Madras.

Clive took with him to India three companies of artillery and 300 infantry. He was instructed to convey them to Bombay, and, joined by all the available troops of the Company and their Marátha allies, to endeavour to wrest the Deccan from French influence. But, just as he was sailing, he discovered that, through royal influence, Colonel Scott of the Engineers, then on the spot, had been nominated to the command, with himself as his second. Not caring to take part in an expedition in which his own voice would not be the decisive voice, Clive was anxious to proceed to take up his government at Fort St. David, when, on his arrival, he learned the death of Colonel Scott. This event recalled him to the original plan. But another complication ensued. Very shortly before he had arranged to march there came the information that the French and English on the Coromandel coast had entered into a treaty, binding on the two nations in India, not to interfere in the warlike operations of native princes. The Deccan project, therefore, had to be abandoned.

Another promptly took its place. A small fort built by the great Sivají on a small island in the harbour of Viziadrug, called by the Muhammadans Gheriá, had for many years past been made the headquarters of a hereditary pirate-chief, known to the world as Angria. This man had perpetrated much evil, seizing territories, plundering towns, committing murders, robbing peaceful vessels, and had made his name feared and detested along the entire length of the Malabar coast. The necessity to punish him had long been admitted alike by the Maráthás and the English. The year preceding the Bombay Government had despatched Commodore Jones with a squadron to attack Angria's possessions. Jones accomplished something, but on arriving before Dábhol he was recalled on the ground that the season was too late for naval operations on that coast.

In the autumn of the following year Admiral Watson came out to assume command of the squadron. It had by this time become more than ever necessary to bring the affair to a definite conclusion, and, as Clive and his troops were on the spot, the Bombay Government, acting with the Maráthás, resolved to despatch the fleet and army to destroy the piratical stronghold. Of the expedition, which reached its destination in February, it is sufficient to state that in two days it destroyed Gheriá. Thence Clive pursued his voyage to the Coromandel coast, and arrived at Fort St. David on the 20th of June.

On that very day there occurred in Calcutta the terrible tragedy of the Black Hole. The Súbahdár of Bengal, Bihár, and Orissa, the Nawáb Siráj-ud-daulá, had, for some fancied grievance, prompted probably by the hope of plunder, seized the English factory at Kásimbázár, near his capital of Murshidábád, plundered it, imprisoned the garrison, and had thence marched against Calcutta. He attacked that settlement on the 15th of June, and after a siege of four days, conducted with great want of leading on the part of the English, obtained possession of it. The English Governor, Mr. Drake, the senior military officer, and many others, had fled for refuge on board the ships in the river Húglí, which immediately had weighed anchor and stood downwards, leaving about 145 men, some of them high in office, and one lady, Mrs. Carey, a prey to the enemy. These were seized and taken before the Nawáb and his commander of the forces, Mír Jafar by name. The Nawáb spoke kindly to them, and ordered that they should be guarded for the night, having no intention whatever, there is the strongest reason to believe, that any harm should befall them. But, owing to the natural cruelty or indifference of their guards, they were thrust, after the departure of the Nawáb, into a small room, about eighteen feet square, ill ventilated, and just capable of receiving them when packed together so closely as to render death certain to the majority. Vainly did they remonstrate; vainly did they send a message to the Nawáb: he was asleep, and no one dared to awaken him. Into that hole they were locked, and in it they remained until the light of day showed that the pestiferous atmosphere had been fatal to all of them except twenty-three. These were then released and taken before the Nawáb. Far from expressing regret for the sufferings of which he had been the involuntary cause, the Nawáb questioned them only about the place in which their treasure had been hidden. For, so far, he had been greatly disappointed at the result of his raid.

The story of the capture of Kásimbázár reached Madras on the 15th of July. The Governor immediately despatched a detachment of 230 European troops for the Húglí, under command of Major Kilpatrick, and this detachment reached its position off the village of Falta on the 2nd of August. For the moment we must leave it there.

It was not until three days after the arrival of Kilpatrick at Falta that information of the Black Hole outrage reached Madras. The position there was critical. The Governor was in daily expectation of hearing that war had been declared with France, and he had already parted with a large detachment of his best troops. The question was whether, in the presence of the possible danger likely to arise from France, he should still further denude the Presidency he administered. The discussion was long. Happily it was finally resolved to despatch to the Húglí every available ship and man. The discussion as to the choice of the commander was still more prolonged; but, after others had insisted on their rights, it was finally determined to commit the command of the land-forces to Clive—who had been summoned from Fort St. George to the consultation—in subordination, however, to Admiral Watson, commanding the squadron. It was not until the second week of October that every detail was settled, nor until the 16th of that month that the fleet sailed for the Húglí. The first ship reached the river, off Falta, the 11th of December. But with the exception of two, one laden with stores, the other grounding off Cape Palmyras, but both of which joined at a later period, the others reached their destination at periods between the 17th and 27th of that month.

The land-forces at the disposal of Clive consisted, including the few remnants of Kilpatrick's detachment,[1] which had suffered greatly from disease, of 830 Europeans, 1200 sipáhís, and a detail of artillery. One ship, containing over 200, had not arrived, and many were on the sick-list.

[1] Orme states that one-half of them had died and that only thirty were fit for duty.

On the 17th of December Watson had written to the Nawáb to demand redress for the losses suffered by the Company, but no answer had been vouchsafed. As soon then as all the ships, the two spoken of excepted, had assembled off Falta, Watson wrote again to inform him that they should take the law into their own hands. On the 27th the fleet weighed anchor, and stood upwards. On the 29th it anchored off Maiápur, a village ten miles below the fort of Baj-baj. It was obvious to both commanders that that fort must be taken; but a difference of opinion occurred as to the mode in which it should be assailed, Clive advocating the proceeding by water, and landing within easy distance of the place, Watson insisting that the troops should land near Maiápur, and march thence. Clive, much against his own opinion, followed this order. Landing, he covered the ten miles, and posted his troops in two villages whence it would be easy to attack the fort on the morrow. The troops, tired with the march, and fearing no enemy, then lay down to sleep. But the Governor of Calcutta, Manikchand, had reached Baj-baj that very morning with a force of 2000 foot and 1500 horse. He had noted, unseen, all the dispositions of Clive, and at nightfall he sallied forth to surprise him. The surprise took effect, in the sense that it placed the English force in very great danger. But it was just one of those situations in which Clive was at his very best. He recognized on the moment that if he were to cause his troops to fall back beyond reach of the enemy's fire, there would be a great danger of a panic. He ordered therefore the line to stand firm where it was, whilst he detached two platoons, from different points, to assail the enemy. One of these suffered greatly from the enemy's fire, but the undaunted conduct of the English in pressing on against superior numbers so impressed the native troops that they fell back, despite the very gallant efforts of their officers to rally them. Clive was then able to form his main line in an advantageous position, and a shot from one of his field-pieces grazing the turban of Manikchand, that chief gave the signal to retire. That night the fort of Baj-baj was taken by a drunken sailor, who, scrambling over the parapet, hailed to his comrades to join him. They found the place abandoned.

On the 2nd of January Calcutta surrendered to Clive. A great altercation took place between that officer and Watson as to the appointment of Governor of that town. Watson had actually nominated Major Eyre Coote, but Clive protested so strongly that, eventually, Watson himself took possession, and then handed the keys to Mr. Drake, the same Drake who had so shamefully abandoned the place at the time of Siráj-ud-daulá's attack. Three days later Clive stormed the important town of Húglí, once a Portuguese settlement, afterwards held by the English, but at the time occupied for the Nawáb.

Meanwhile that prince, collecting his army, numbering about 40,000 men of sorts, was marching to recover his lost conquest. To observe him Clive took a position at Kásipur, a suburb of Calcutta, now the seat of a gun-factory. As the Nawáb approached, the English leader made as though he would attack him, but finding him prepared, he drew back to await a better opportunity. By the 3rd of February the entire army of the Nawáb had encamped just beyond the regular line of the Maráthá ditch. Thither Clive despatched two envoys to negotiate with the Nawáb, but finding that they were received with contumely and insult, he borrowed some sailors from the Admiral, and, obtaining his assent to the proposal, resolved to attack him before dawn of the next day. Accordingly at three o'clock on the morning of the 4th of February, Clive broke up, and, under cover of one of those dense fogs so common in Bengal about Christmastime, penetrated within the Nawáb's camp. Again was he in imminent danger. For when, at six o'clock, the fog lifted for a few seconds, he found the enemy's cavalry massed along his flank. They were as surprised at the proximity as was Clive himself, and a sharp volley sent them scampering away. The fog again descended: Clive knew not exactly where he was; his men were becoming confused; and Clive knew that the step from confusion to panic was but a short one. But he never lost his presence of mind. He kept his men together; and when, at eight o'clock, there was a second lifting of the fog, and he recognized that he was in the very centre of the enemy's camp, he marched boldly forward, and not only extricated his troops, but so impressed the Nawáb that he drew off his army, and on the 9th signed a treaty, by which he covenanted to grant to the English more than their former privileges, and promised the restoration of the property he had seized at the capture of Calcutta. This accident of the fog and its consequences form, indeed, the keynote to the events that followed. The circumstances connected with it completely dominated the mind of the Nawáb; instilled into his mind so great a fear of the English leader that he came entirely under his influence, and, though often kicking against it, remained under it to the end. This feeling was increased when, some weeks later, Clive, learning that war had been declared between France and England, attacked and conquered the French settlement of Chandranagar (March 23), in spite of the Nawáb's prohibition. He displayed it to the world a little later, by dismissing from his court and exiling to a place a hundred miles distant from it a small detachment of French troops which he had there in his pay, commanded by the Law who had so misconducted the siege of Trichinopoli, and by recalling his army from Plassey, where he had posted it, to a point nearer to his capital.

Of Siráj-ud-daulá something must be said. The province which he ruled from his then capital of Murshidábád had been one of the great fiefs which the dissolution of the Mughal Empire had affected. The family which had ruled it in 1739 had had the stamp of approval from Delhi. But when the invasion of Nadír Sháh in that year overthrew for the time the authority of the Mughal, an officer named Alí Vardi Khán, who had risen from the position of a menial servant to be Governor of Bihár, rose in revolt, defeated and slew the representative of the family nominated by the Mughals in a battle at Gheriá, in January, 1741, and proclaimed himself Súbahdár. Alí Vardi Khán was a very able man. Having bribed the shadow sitting on the throne of Akbar and Aurangzeb to recognize him as Súbahdár of Bengal, Bihár, and Orissa, he ruled wisely and well. On his death in 1756 he had been succeeded by his youthful grandson, the Siráj-ud-daulá, who, as we have seen, had come, so fatally for himself, under the influence of Clive.

For all the actions of Clive at this period prove that he was resolved to place matters in Bengal on such a footing as would render impossible atrocities akin to that of the Black Hole. Were he to quit Bengal, he felt, after accomplishing the mission on which he had been sent, and that mission only, what security was there that the Súbahdár would not return to wreak a vengeance the more bitter from the mortifications he had had to endure? No, there was but one course he could safely pursue. He must place the Company's affairs on a solid and secure footing. Already he had begun to feel that such a footing was impossible so long as Siráj-ud-daulá remained ruler of the three provinces. As time went on the idea gathered strength, receiving daily, as it did, fresh vitality from the discovery that among the many noblemen and wealthy merchants who surrounded the Súbahdár there were many ready to betray him, to play into his own hand, to combine with himself as against a common foe.

Soon his difficulty was to choose the man with whom he should ally himself. Yár Lutf Khán, a considerable noble, and a divisional commander of the Siráj-ud-daulá's army, made, through Mr. Watts, the English agent at Kásimbázár, the first offer of co-operation, on the sole condition that he should become Súbahdár. It was followed by another from a man occupying a still higher position, from the Bakhshí, or Commander-in-chief, Mír Jafar Khán. This Clive accepted, receiving at the same time offers of adhesion from Rájá Duláb Ráo; from other leading nobles, and from the influential bankers and merchants of Murshidábád.

Then began those negotiations one detail of which has done so much to stain the name of the great soldier. The contracting parties employed in their negotiations one Aminchand, a Calcutta merchant of considerable wealth, great address, unbounded cunning, and absolutely without a conscience. When the plot was at its thickest, this man—who was likewise betraying the confidence which Siráj-ud-daulá bestowed upon him, when the least word would have rendered it abortive—informed the Calcutta Select Committee, through Mr. Watts, that unless twenty lakhs of rupees were secured to him in the instrument which formed the bond of the confederates, he would at once disclose to the Súbahdár the plans of the conspirators. The inevitable result of this disclosure would have been ruin to all the conspirators; death to many of them. To baffle the greed of this blackmailer, Clive caused two copies of the document to be drawn up, from one of which the name of Aminchand was omitted. To disarm his suspicions, the false document was shown him. This latter all the contracting parties had signed, with the exception of Admiral Watson, who demurred, but who, according to the best recollection of Clive in his evidence before the Committee of the House of Commons, did not object to have his name attached thereto by another.[2]

[2] These are the facts of the transaction: they will be commented upon in a future page. Vide comment near the end of Chapter X.

Space would fail were I to detail the various modes employed by the confederates to produce on the mind of Siráj-ud-daulá the conviction that his only safety lay in battle with the English. He had tried many methods to escape the dilemma, to rid himself of the heavy hand of Clive. He had made overtures to Bussy at Haidarábád; to the Maráthás; to the Court of Delhi; to the Nawáb-Wazir of Oudh. But every proposed combination had fallen through. He had quarrelled with Mír Jafar, with his chief nobles, with the bankers. He had suspected treachery, but had never been quite certain. At last, on the thirteenth of June, information was brought to him that the English agent, Mr. Watts, and his subordinates, had fled from Kásimbázár, after an interview with Mír Jafar, at the time in his disfavour. Then he gave way: then he realized that, without the aid of his nobles, he was helpless: then he guessed the whole plot; the schemes of Clive; the treason of his own people: then he turned to Mír Jafar for reconciliation, imploring him not to abandon him in his distress. Mír Jafar and the other nobles, most of whom were in the plot, all swore fealty and obedience, Mír Jafar leading the way. They would risk everything for the Súbahdár. They would drive back the cursed English, and free Bengal from their influence. Recovering his equanimity from these assurances, Siráj-ud-daulá ordered his army to march to an intrenched camp he had prepared near the village of Plassey, in the island of Kásimbázár,[3] twenty-two miles distant. There was some difficulty regarding the arrears of pay of his men, failing the settlement of which they refused to march. But, with friendly assistancethis difficulty was overcome; the army set out three days later for its destination, and arrived in the intrenched camp on the 21st of June.

[3] Kásimbázár is called an island because whilst the base of the triangle which composes it is watered by the Ganges, the western side, on which lies Plassey, is watered by the Bhágirathí; the eastern by the Jalangí.

I propose now briefly to record the movements of Clive: then to describe the decisive battle which followed his arrival on the island.

CHAPTER IX
THE BATTLE OF PLASSEY

Meanwhile Clive had made every preparation for the advance of his army. A considerable portion of it had been stationed at Chandranagar. To that place he despatched on the 12th of June all the soldiers available, and 150 sailors lent him by the Admiral, leaving Calcutta guarded by a few sick Europeans, some sipáhís to look after the French prisoners, and a few gunners to man the guns on the ramparts. On the 13th he quitted Chandranagar, the Europeans, with the guns, munitions, and stores, proceeding by water in 200 boats, towed by natives against the stream, the sipáhís marching along the right bank of the river, on the highroad made by the Mughal Government from Húglí to Patna.[1] The force consisted, all told, of about 900 Europeans, 200 men of mixed native and Portuguese blood who served with the Europeans, a small detail of lascars, and 2100 sipáhís. The artillery consisted of eight six-pounders and two small howitzers.

[1] Vide Broome's *History of the Bengal Army*, p. 137.

The day after the force had set out Clive despatched to the Súbahdár a communication tantamount to a declaration of war; and he proceeded, as he approached the enemy's camp, to act as though such a declaration had been accepted. On the 16th he reached Paltí, a town on the western bank of the Kásimbázár river about six miles above its junction with the Jalangí. Twelve miles higher up he came within striking distance of Katwá, the Governor of which was supposed to be one of the conspirators. Clive, expecting that the opposition would not be serious, despatched to occupy it, on the 17th, 200 Europeans and 500 sipáhis, under Major Eyre Coote. But either the Governor had changed his mind or he had only feigned compliance, for he prepared to resist Coote's attack. Coote at once made preparations for an assault, and took such dispositions, that the garrison, recognizing the futility of resistance, and fearing to be cut off, evacuated the place, leaving large supplies in the hands of the victors.

The next day, the 18th, a terrific storm raging, the force halted. The day following, Clive, who had committed himself to the enterprise mainly on the conviction that Mír Jafar would support him, received a letter from that nobleman, informing him that he had feigned reconciliation with the Súbahdár and had taken an oath not to assist the English, but adding that 'the purport of his convention with them must be carried into execution.' This strange letter from the man upon whose co-operation he particularly depended led Clive to doubt whether, after all, Mír Jafar might not betray him. Under this possibility, the sense of the extreme danger of the enterprise in which he was engaged revealed itself to him more clearly than it had ever presented itself before. To cross an unfordable river in the face of a vastly superior enemy, at a distance of 150 miles from all support, would, he felt, be a most hazardous undertaking. Should Mír Jafar be faithless to him, as he had appeared to be to his master, and should the English force be defeated, there would scarcely survive a man to tell the tale. Again would Calcutta be in jeopardy—this time probably beyond redemption. Under the influence of such thoughts he resolved not to cross the river until he should receive from Mír Jafar more definite assurances.

The next day, the 20th, a messenger arrived from his agent, Mr. Watts, who was then at Kalná, carrying a letter to the effect that before he quitted Murshidábád he had been engaged in an interview with Mír Jafar and his son, when there entered some emissaries of the Súbahdár; that, in the presence of these, Mír Jafar had denounced Mr. Watts as a spy, and had threatened to destroy the English if they should attempt to cross the Bhágírathí. This letter decided Clive. He resolved to summon a Council of War.

There came to that Council, about noon of the 21st of June, the following officers: Colonel Clive, Majors Kilpatrick and Grant, Captains Gaupp, Rumbold, Fischer, Palmer, Le Beaume, Waggonner, Corneille, and Jennings, Captain-Lieutenants Parshaw and Molitore;— Major Eyre Coote, Captains Alexander Grant, Cudmore, Armstrong, Muir, Campbell, and Captain-Lieutenant Carstairs. The question submitted to them was: 'whether under existing circumstances, and without other assistance, it would be prudent to cross the river and come to action at once with the Nawáb, or whether they should fortify themselves at Katwá, and wait till the monsoon was over, when the Maráthás or some other country power might be induced to join them.' Contrary to the usual custom, Clive spoke first, the others following according to seniority. Clive spoke and voted against immediate action. He was supported by the twelve officers whose names immediately follow his own name in the list I have given, and opposed by the owners of the seven last names, Major Eyre Coote speaking very emphatically in favour of action; the majority of the Council, we thus see, siding with Clive.

The subsequent career of Eyre Coote, especially in Southern India, proved very clearly that as a commander in the field he fell far short of Robert Clive, but on this occasion he was the wiser of the two. Some years later Clive, giving his evidence before a Select Committee of the House of Commons, emphatically stated that had he abided by the decision of the Council it would have caused the ruin of the East India Company. As it was, he reconsidered his vote the moment the Council was over. It is said that he sat down under a clump of trees, and began to turn over in his mind the arguments on both sides. He was still sitting when a despatch from Mír Jafar[2] reached him, containing favourable assurances. Clive then resolved to fight. All doubt had disappeared from his mind. He was again firm, self-reliant, confident. Meeting Eyre Coote as he returned to his quarters, he simply informed him that he had changed his mind and intended to fight, and then proceeded to dictate in his own tent the orders for the advance.

[2] Vide Ives's *Voyage and Historical Narrative*, p. 150. Mr. Ives was surgeon of the *Kent* during the expedition to Bengal, and was a great friend of Admiral Watson.

At sunrise on the 22nd the force commenced the passage of the river. By four o'clock it was safe on the other side. Here a letter was received from Mír Jafar, informing Clive of the contemplated movements of the Nawáb. Clive replied that he 'would march to Plassey without delay, and would the next morning advance six miles further to the village of Dáudpur, but if Mír Jafar did not join him there, he would make peace with the Nawáb.' Two hours later, about sunset, he commenced his march amid a storm of heavy rain which wetted the men to the skin. In all respects, indeed, the march was particularly trying, for the recent rains had inundated the country, and for eight hours the troops had to follow the line of the river, the water constantly reaching their waists. They reached Plassey, a distance of fifteen miles, at one o'clock on the morning of the 23rd of June, and lay down to sleep in a mango-grove, the sound of drums and other music in the camp of the Nawáb solacing rather than disturbing them. The Súbahdár had reached his headquarters twelve hours before them.

The mango-tope in which the English were resting was but a mile distant from the intrenched position occupied by Siráj-ud-daulá's army. It was about 800 yards in length and 300 in breadth, the trees planted in regular rows. All round it was a bank of earth, forming a good breastwork. Beyond this was a ditch choked with weeds and brambles. The length of the grove was nearly diagonal to the river, the north-west angle being little more than 50 yards from the bank, whilst at the south-west corner it was more than 200 yards distant. A little in advance, on the bank of the river, stood a hunting-box belonging to the Nawáb, encompassed by a wall of masonry. In this, during the night, Clive placed 200 Europeans and 300 natives, with two field-pieces. But in the morning he withdrew the greater part of them.[3] He had with him 950 European infantry and artillery, 200 topasses, men of mixed race, armed and equipped as Europeans, 50 sailors with seven midshipmen attached, 2100 sipáhís, a detail of lascars, and the field-pieces already mentioned.

[3] Vide Orme's *History of India*, and Broome's *History of the Bengal Army*.

On the spot which the Nawáb had selected for his intrenched camp the river makes a bend in the form of a horseshoe, with the points much contracted, forming a peninsula of about three miles in circumference, the neck of which was less than a quarter of a mile in breadth. The intrenchment commenced a little below the southern point of this gorge, resting on the river, and extending inland for about 200 yards, and sweeping thence round to the north for about three miles. At this angle was a redoubt, on which the enemy had mounted several pieces of cannon. About 300 yards to the eastward of this redoubt was a hillock covered with jungle, and about 800 yards to the south, nearer Clive's grove, was a tank, and 100 yards further south was a second and larger one. Both of these were surrounded by large mounds of earth, and, with the hillock, formed important positions for either army to occupy. The Súbahdár's army was encamped partly in this peninsula, partly in rear of the intrenchment. He had 50,000 infantry of sorts, 18,000 horse of a better quality, and 53 guns, mostly 32, 24, and 18-pounders. The infantry was armed chiefly with matchlocks, swords, pikes, bows and arrows, and possessed little or no discipline; the cavalry was well-trained and well-mounted; the guns were mounted on large platforms, furnished with wheels, and drawn by forty or fifty yoke of powerful oxen, assisted by elephants. But the most efficient portion of his force was a small party of forty to fifty Frenchmen, commanded by M. St. Frais, formerly one of the Council of Chandranagar. This party had attached to it four light field-pieces.[4]

[4] For these details see Orme, Broome, Clive's *Evidence before the Committee of the House of Commons*, Clive's *Report to the Court of Directors*, Sir Eyre Coote's *Narrative*, and Ives's *Voyage and Historical Narrative*. The account which follows is based entirely on these authorities.

At daybreak on the 23rd of June the Nawáb moved his entire army out of the intrenchment and advanced towards the position occupied by Clive, the several corps marching in compact order. In front was St. Frais, who took post at the larger tank, that nearest Clive's grove. On a line to his right, near the river, were a couple of heavy guns, under the orders of a native officer. Behind these two advanced parties, and within supporting distance, was a chosen body of 5000 horse and 7000 foot, under the immediate command of the Nawáb's most faithful general, Mír Madan.[5] The rest of the Nawáb's army extended in a curve, its right resting on the hillock near the camp; thence sweeping round in dense columns of horse and foot to the eastward of the south-east angle of the grove. Here, nearest to the English, were placed the troops of Mír Jafar, then those of Yár Lutf Khán, beyond these Rájá Duláb Rám. The English within the grove were thus almost surrounded by the river and the enemy; but in view of the promised treachery of Mír Jafar, the greatest danger was to be apprehended from their immediate front, viz. from St. Frais, with his little body of Frenchmen, and from Mír Madan.

[5] See Elliot's *History of India*, vol. viii. p. 428.

From the roof of the hunting-house Clive watched his enemy take up the positions which would hold him, if their generals were true to their master, in a vice. 'They approached apace,' he wrote in a letter of July 26 to the Secret Committee of the Court of Directors, 'and by six began to attack us with a number of heavy cannon, supported by the whole army, and continued to play on us very briskly for several hours, during which our situation was of the utmost service to us, being lodged in a large grove, with good mud banks. To succeed in an attempt on their cannon was next to impossible, as they were planted in a manner round us, and at considerable distances from each other. We therefore remained quiet in our post, in expectation of a successful attack upon their camp at night. About noon the enemy drew off their artillery and returned to their camp.'

So far, up to mid-day, we have the outline of the fight as narrated by Clive; it is, however, but an outline. It would seem that the action commenced by a discharge of one of the four guns of St. Frais. This discharge killed one and wounded another of the men of the European battalion. Immediately afterwards the whole of the enemy's guns opened fire, but their shots flew high, and did but little mischief. Clive meanwhile had drawn up his troops in line in front of the grove, their left resting on the hunting-box, with the exception of two guns and two howitzers which he had posted at some brick-kilns some 200 yards in front of the hunting-box spoken of. These, as soon as the enemy opened, replied promptly and effectively. The remaining six guns, placed three on each flank of the European battalion which formed the centre of his line, answered the heavy batteries of the enemy, but, from their small calibre, made but little impression.

After a cannonade of half an hour, the English having lost ten Europeans and twenty sipáhís in killed and wounded, Clive withdrew them under shelter of the grove, leaving one detachment at the brick-kilns, another at the hunting-box. This retrograde movement greatly encouraged the enemy. They brought their guns much nearer, and their fire became more vigorous and sustained. But its effect was less fatal, for the English troops were protected by the trees and the mud bank, and, sitting down, were but little exposed. This warfare continued till about eleven o'clock, the casualties being far greater on the side of the Nawáb's army than among the English. Then Clive summoned his principal officers to a conference, and it was resolved that the troops should occupy their existing positions until midnight, and should then attack the Nawáb's camp. We may regard the close of the conference as occurring about the same time as the withdrawal of the enemy's artillery indicated by Clive in the above extract from his despatch.

For, scarcely was the conference over, than the skies poured down a fierce shower, such as occurs often during the rainy season, which lasted an hour. Then it was that the enemy's artillery fire slackened by degrees almost to the point of ceasing, for the rain had damaged their ammunition, left almost completely without cover. Clive had been more careful of his powder, so that when the enemy's horse, believing the English guns as powerless as their own, advanced towards the grove to charge, they were received with a fire which emptied many a saddle, and sent them reeling back. In this charge Mír Madan, previously referred to, was killed.[6]

[6] Elliot states, on the authority of the J'ami'ut Taw'ari'kh, that he was accidentally struck by a cannon-ball. *History of India*, vol. viii. p. 427.

The death of this brave and faithful soldier greatly disheartened the Súbahdár. He sent for Mír Jafar, and implored him to remain faithful to his oath. Taking off his turban and casting it at the feet of his uncle,[7] he exclaimed in humble tones, 'Jafar, that turban thou must defend.' Mír Jafar promised, but instead of performing, the degenerate Muhammadan returned to his confederates and sent a despatch to Clive, informing him of all that had passed, and begging him to push on immediately, or, if that were impossible, not to fail to attack during the night. His letter did not reach Clive till late in the evening. Meanwhile other influences had been at work to bring about a similar result.

[7] Mír Jafar had married the sister of Alí Vardi Khán, the Nawáb's father.

It is impossible not to feel sympathy for the youthful prince, surrounded by traitors, his one true adherent killed. Scarcely had Mír Jafar quitted him when there came to him another traitor, Rájá Duláb Rám, who commanded the army corps nearest to the position he had taken. The Rájá found his master in a state of great agitation. The English were showing themselves in the open; his own men were giving way; hope was vanishing quickly. Instead of encouraging the Súbahdár to fight it out, the treacherous Rájá gave fuel to his fears, told him the day was lost, and urged him to flee to Murshidábád. In an evil hour for his dynasty and for himself, Siráj-ud-daulá yielded to his persuasions, and, ordering his troops to retire within the intrenchment, mounted a swift dromedary, and fled, accompanied by 2000 horsemen, to his capital.

It was then two o'clock. The first hour since Clive's conference had been marked by the heavy rain; the second by the repulse of the Súbahdár's horsemen; the following up of the repulsed attack; the conversations of the Súbahdár with his two treacherous generals. By two o'clock the enemy's attack had completely ceased, and they were observed yoking their oxen preparatory to withdrawing within the intrenchment as the Súbahdár had ordered. There remained only on the ground that body of forty gallant Frenchmen under St. Frais, whom I have described as occupying the ground about the larger tank, that nearest to the grove. The post was an important one, for from it the English could have taken the retreating enemy in flank, and have inflicted heavy loss upon them. St. Frais was nearly isolated, but he, too, had seen the advantage the English would derive from occupying the position, and, faithful amid the faithless, he, with the gallantry of his nation, resolved to defend it until it should be no longer defensible.

There was with the army a very gallant officer, Major James Kilpatrick, who had greatly distinguished himself in Southern India, and who, on this occasion, commanded the Company's troops. Kilpatrick had noted the firm front displayed by St. Frais, the great advantage to be derived from occupying the position he held, the disadvantage of leaving him to hold it whilst the English force should advance. He resolved, then, to expel him: so sending word to Clive of his intentions, and of the reason which prompted his action, he marched with two companies towards St. Frais.

Clive, meanwhile, seeing the enemy's attack broken, yet deeming it better, not having received Mír Jafar's letter, to wait till the sun should have descended before making the decisive attack, had proceeded to the hunting-box to rest after so many hours of fatigue and excitement, to be followed, he believed, by many more, having first given orders that he should be informed of any change that might occur in the enemy's position. He was there when the message of Kilpatrick reached him. Rising, he hurried to the spot, met Kilpatrick as he was advancing to the assault, reprimanded him for having taken such a step without orders, but seeing him so far forward, he took himself the command of the detachment, sending back Kilpatrick to the grove to bring the remainder of the troops. When St. Frais recognized the earnestness of the English, and that he was entirely without support, he evacuated the post, and retreated to the redoubt at the corner of the intrenchment. There he placed his guns ready for action.[8]

[8] This episode is not specially mentioned by Clive, but it rests on irrefragable evidence. Vide Orme, vol. ii. p. 176: see also Sir Eyre Coote's *Narrative*, also Malcolm's *Life of Lord Clive*, vol. i. p. 260.

Meanwhile, whilst the English force was thus advancing, the army corps commanded by Mír Jafar was observed to linger behind the rest of the retreating enemy. It was noticed, further, that when it had advanced almost abreast of the northern line of the grove, it faced to its left and advanced in that direction. For a time it seemed to the English officers as though the troops composing it were about to make a raid on their baggage, and a party with a field-piece was sent forward to check them. The corps then halted, remained so for a time, then slowly retired, taking, however, a direction which led it apart from the other corps of the enemy. We shall return to them in a few moments.

Whilst this corps was executing the manoeuvre I have described, Clive had advanced to a position whence he could cannonade the enemy's camp. The effect of this fire was to cause great loss and confusion amongst the troops of the Súbahdár, at the same time that the English, giving, by their advance, their flank to the French in the redoubt, suffered also. To put an end to this cross-fire Clive saw that the one remedy was to storm the redoubt. He was unwilling, however, to risk his troops in a severe contest with the French so long as the army corps, the movements of which I have described in the preceding paragraph, should continue to occupy its apparently threatening position. That corps might be the corps of Mír Jafar, but there was no certainty that it was so, for Clive had not then received Mír Jafar's letter, nor was he aware of the flight of the Nawáb. It was just at this critical moment that he observed the corps in question making the retrograde movement I have referred to. Then all doubt was over in his mind. It must, he was convinced, be the corps of his adherent. Certain now that he would not be molested, he hurled his troops against the redoubt and the hillock to the east of it. St. Frais displayed a bold front, but, abandoned almost immediately by his native allies, and deeming it wiser to preserve his handful of Europeans for another occasion, he evacuated the redoubt, leaving his field-pieces behind him. His resistance was the last opposition offered to the English. The clocks struck five as he fell back, thus tolling the memorable hour which gave to England the richest province in India; which imposed upon her the necessity to advance upwards from its basis until she should reach the rocky region called with some show of reason the 'Glacis of the Fortress of Hindustán.'

Just as the beaten and betrayed army was moving off with its impedimenta, its elephants, its camels, leaving to be scrambled for an enormous mass of baggage, stores, cattle, and camp equipage, Clive received messengers from Mír Jafar requesting an interview. Clive replied by appointing a meeting for the morrow at Dáudpur, a village twenty miles to the south of Murshidábád. Thither the bulk of the troops, their spirits cheered by the promise made them that they would receive a liberal donation in money, marched that evening; whilst a detachment under Eyre Coote went forward in pursuit, to prevent the enemy from rallying. After a short halt, to enable the commissariat to exchange their small and worn-out bullocks for the splendid oxen of the Súbahdár, the troops pressed on, and at eight o'clock the entire force was united at Dáudpur.

Such was the battle of Plassey. The loss of the English force was extremely small, amounting to seven Europeans and sixteen sipáhís killed, and thirteen Europeans and thirty-six sipáhís wounded. No officer was killed: two were wounded, but their names are not recorded. A midshipman of the *Kent*, Shoreditch by name, was shot in the thigh, whilst doing duty with the artillery. The enemy's casualties were far greater. It was calculated to be, in killed and wounded, about a thousand, including many officers. They had been far more exposed than the English. Writing, in the letter already referred to, of the phases of the action between two and five o'clock, Clive states that their horse exposed themselves a great deal; that 'many of them were killed, amongst the rest four or five officers of the first distinction.'

Clive had gained his victory. We have now to record the use that he made of it.

CHAPTER X
HOW CLIVE DEALT WITH THE SPOILS OF PLASSEY: HIS DEALINGS WITH MÍR JAFAR; WITH THE PRINCES OF SOUTHERN INDIA; WITH THE DUTCH

The following morning Clive despatched Mr. Scrafton and Omar Beg[1] to escort Mír Jafar to his camp. The time had arrived when one at least of the spoils of Plassey was to be distributed.

[1] Omar Beg was a confidential agent of Mír Jafar, attached to Clive's person.

Long previous to the battle Clive had received various proposals from the three general officers who had commanded the three principal army corps at Plassey. First, Yár Lutf Khán had made him a bid, his main condition being that he should be proclaimed Súbahdár.[2] Then Mír Jafar outbad him, bringing with him Rájá Duláb Rám, who would be content with the office of Finance Minister under the Mír. It had been arranged that whilst Mír Jafar should be proclaimed Súbahdár of the three provinces, he should confirm to the English all the advantages ceded by Siráj-ud-daulá in the preceding February; should grant to the Company all the lands lying to the south of Calcutta, together with a slip of ground, 600 yards wide, all round the outside of the Marátha Ditch;[3] should cede all the French factories and establishments in the province; should pledge himself that neither he nor his successors in the office of Súbahdár should erect fortifications below the town of Húglí; whilst he and they should give to, and require from, the English, support in case of hostilities from any quarter. Mír Jafar covenanted likewise to make very large payments to the Company and others under the name of restitution for the damages they had suffered since the first attack on Calcutta; others also under the title of gratification for services to be rendered in placing him on the *masnad*.[4] In the former category were reckoned one karor, or ten millions, of rupees to be paid to the Company; ten lakhs to the native inhabitants of Calcutta, seven lakhs to the Armenians. Under the second head payments were to be made to the army, the squadron, and the members of the Special Committee of Calcutta, to the extent noted below.[5]

[2] Súbahdár was the correct official title of the governor, or, as he is popularly styled, the Nawáb, of Bengal.

[3] It must be recollected that in those days the Maráthás were regarded as serious and formidable enemies. It was against their depredations that the ditch round Calcutta, known as the 'Marátha Ditch,' had been dug.

[4] *Masnad*, a cushion, signifying the seat of supreme authority.

[5] The Squadron was to receive 2,500,000 rupees; the Army, the same; Mr. Drake, Governor of Calcutta (the same who had quitted Calcutta and his companions to take shelter on board ship at the time of Siráj-ud-daulá's attack), 280,000; Colonel Clive, as second in the Select Committee (appointed before the war to negotiate with Mír Jafar), 280,000; Major Kilpatrick, Mr. Watts, and Mr. Becher, as members of the said Committee, 240,000 each. I may here state in anticipation that, in addition to these sums, the following private donations were subsequently given, viz.: to Clive, 1,600,000 rupees; to Watts, 300,000; to the six members of Council, 100,000 each; to Walsh, Clive's secretary and paymaster to the Madras troops, 500,000; to Scrafton, 200,000; to Lushington, 50,000; to Major A. Grant, commanding the detachment of H.M.'s 39th regiment, 100,000.

The first of these contracts, now become binding, was to be carried out on the morning of the 24th of June, at the interview between the two principal parties, Clive and Mír Jafar. It has occurred to me that the reader may possibly care to know something more, little though it be, of the antecedents of this general, who, to his own subsequent unhappiness, betrayed his master for his own gain.

Mír Muhammad Jafar was a nobleman whose family had settled in Bihár. He had taken service under, had become a trusted officer of, Alí Vardi Khán, the father of Siráj-ud-daulá, and had married his sister. On his death, he had been made Bakhshí, or Commander-in-chief, of the army, and, in that capacity, had commanded it when it took Calcutta in June, 1756.[6] Between himself and his wife's nephew, Siráj-ud-daulá, there had never been any cordiality. The latter, with the insolence of untamed and uneducated youth, had kicked against the authority of his uncle; had frequently insulted him; and had even removed him from his office. Mír Jafar had felt these slights bitterly. Living, as he was, in an age of revolution, dynasties falling about him, the very throne of Delhi the appanage of the strongest, he felt no compunction in allying himself with the foreigner to remove from the throne—for it was virtually a throne—of Murshidábád the man who alternately insulted and fawned upon him. Little did he know, little even did he reck, the price he would have to pay. Fortunately for his peace of mind at the moment the future was mercifully hidden from him. But those who are familiar with the history of Bengal after the first departure thence of Clive for England will admit that never did treason so surely find its own punishment as did the treason of Mír Jafar.

[6] There can be no doubt about this. 'About five o'clock the Nawáb entered the fort, carried in an open litter, attended by Mír Jafar Khán, his Bakhshí or General-in-chief, and the rest of his principal officers.' He was present when the English were brought before the Nawáb: vide Broome, p. 66. Orme, vol. ii. p. 73, makes a similar statement.

But he is approaching now, with doubt and anxiety as to his reception, the camp in which he is to receive from his confederate the reward of treason, or reproaches for his want of efficient co-operation on the day preceding. On reaching the camp, writes the contemporary historian of the period,[7] 'he alighted from his elephant, and the guard drew out and rested their arms, to receive him with the highest honours. Not knowing the meaning of this compliment, he drew back, as if he thought it a preparation to his destruction; but Colonel Clive, advancing hastily, embraced him, and saluted him Súbahdár of Bengal, Bihár, and Orissa, which removed his fears.' They discoursed then for about an hour. Clive pressed upon him the great necessity of proceeding at once to Murshidábád to look after Siráj-ud-daulá, and to prevent the plunder of the treasury. The new Súbahdár assented, and, returning to his army, set out and arrived at the capital the same evening. Clive, having sent friendly letters to the other chief conspirators, made a short march of six miles to the village of Baptá, and encamped there for the evening. At noon the day following he proceeded to Madhupur, whence he despatched Messrs. Watts and Walsh, with an escort of 100 sipáhís, to arrange for the payments noted in a preceding page. These soon found that the treasury was not at the moment equal to the demand. They arranged accordingly that one moiety should be paid down: of this moiety two-thirds in hard coin, one-third in jewels and plate; that the second moiety should be discharged by three equal payments, extending over three years.

[7] Orme, vol. ii. p. 178.

Whilst these negotiations were progressing, Clive, having ascertained that the other chief conspirators had accepted the terms offered to them, entered the city of Murshidábád (July 29), attended by 200 Europeans and 300 sipáhís, and took up his quarters in the palace of Murádbágh, his followers encamping in the garden attached to it. Here he was waited upon by Míran, the eldest son of Mír Jafar, and with him he proceeded to the Súbahdár's palace, where Mír Jafar and his principal officers were waiting to receive him. Clive, after saluting Mír Jafar, led him to the *masnad*, and, despite some affected unwillingness on the part of the Mír, seated him upon it, hailed him with the usual forms as Súbahdár, offering at the same time a nazar of 100 *ashrafís*.[8] He then, through an interpreter, addressed the assembled nobles, congratulated them on the change of masters, and urged them to be faithful to Mír Jafar. The usual ceremonies followed, and the new ruler was publicly proclaimed throughout the city.

[8] The value of an *ashrafía*, at a later period called by the English 'Gold Muhr,' was about 1*l.* 11*s.* 8*d.* A 'nazar' is a gift offered and received when people of rank pay their respects to a prince. It is more properly called 'Nazráná.'

It is impossible to quit this subject without recording, as briefly as possible, the fate of the relative Mír Jafar had betrayed and supplanted. Siráj-ud-daulá, fleeing, as we have seen, from the field of Plassey, had reached Murshidábád the same night. The next morning the news of the total rout of his army reached him. He remained in his palace till dusk, then, accompanied by his favourite wife, he embarked on a boat, hoping to find refuge in the camp of M. Law, who was advancing from Bhágalpur. But at Rájmahál the strength of the rowers gave out, and the young prince rested for the night in the buildings of a deserted garden. There he was discovered, and, taken back, was made over to Mír Jafar. The interview which followed will recall to the English historical student the scene between James II and the Duke of Monmouth. There was the same vain imploring for life on the one side, the same inexorable refusal on the other. That same night Siráj-ud-daulá was stabbed to death in his cell.

Another scene, scarcely less revolting in its details, had occurred the preceding day. I have mentioned the two treaties made by the conspirators, the one the real treaty, the other a counterpart, drawn up to deceive Aminchand. In the distribution of the plunder it had become necessary to disclose the truth to the wily Bengal speculator. For him there need be but little pity. Entrusted with the secrets of the conspirators, he had threatened to betray them unless twenty lakhs of rupees should be secured to him in the general agreement. He was, in a word—to use an expression much in use at the present day—a 'blackmailer.' Clive and the officers with whom he was acting thought it justifiable to deceive such a man. The hour of his awakening had now arrived. The two treaties were produced, and Aminchand was somewhat brutally informed by Mr. Scrafton that the treaty in which his name appeared was a sham; that he was to have nothing. The sudden shock is said to have alienated his reason. But if so, the alienation was only temporary. He proceeded on a pilgrimage to Malda, and for a time abstained from business. But the old records of Calcutta show that he soon returned to his trade, for his name appears in many of the transactions in which the English were interested after the departure of Clive.

Nor was the dealing with Aminchand the only matter connected with the distribution of the spoil which caused ill-feeling. There had been much bitterness stirred up in the army by the fact that the sailors who had fought at Plassey should receive their share of the amount promised to the navy in addition to that which would accrue to them as fighting men. A mixed Committee, composed of representatives of each branch of the military service, had decided against the claims of the sailors to draw from both sources, and Clive was appealed to to confirm it. But Clive, who, in matters of discipline, was unbending, overruled the decision of the Committee, placed its leader, Captain Armstrong, under arrest, and dissolved the Committee. In a dignified letter Clive pointed out to the Committee their error, and drew from them an apology. But the feeling rankled. It displayed itself a little later in the acquittal of Captain Armstrong by a court-martial. In other respects the distribution of the money was harmful, for it led to excesses among officers and men, and, consequently, to a large increase of mortality.

Meanwhile the new Súbahdár began to find that the State-cushion was not altogether a bed of roses. The enormous sums demanded by his English allies, and by other adherents, had forced him, as soon as Clive had left for Calcutta, to apply the screw to the wealthier of his new subjects. Even his fellow-conspirators felt the burden. Rájá Duláb Rám, whom he had made Finance Minister, with the right to appropriate to himself five per cent. on all payments made by the Treasury, retired in dudgeon to his own palace, summoned his friends, and refused all intercourse with Mír Jafar. The Rájá of Purniah and the Governor of Bihár went into rebellion. The disaffection reached even the distant city of Dháká, where the son of Sarfaráz, the representative of the ancient family ruling in Bengal, lived in retirement and hope. Under these circumstances Mír Jafar, though he well knew what it would cost him, made an application for assistance to Clive.

The English leader had expected the application. He had recognized long before that, in the East, power depends mainly on the length of the purse, and that, from having exhausted his treasury, Mír Jafar would be forced to sue to him *in forma pauperis*. Clive had studied the situation in all its aspects. The blow he had given to native rule by the striking down of the late Súbahdár had rendered absolute government, such as that exercised by Siráj-ud-daulá, impossible. Thenceforth it had become indispensable that the English should supervise the native rule, leaving to the Súbahdár the initiative and the semblance. Clive had reason to believe that whilst Mír Jafar would be unwilling to play such a rôle, he would yet, under pressure, play it. He had seen that the new ruler was so enamoured of the paraphernalia of power that, rather than renounce it, he would agree to whatever terms he might impose which would secure for him nominal authority. There was but one point regarding which he had doubts, and that was whether the proud Muhammadan nobles to whom, in the days of the glories of the Mughal empire, great estates had been granted in Bengal, would tamely submit to a system which would give to the Western invaders all the actual power, and to the chief of their own class and religion only the outer show.

The application from Mír Jafar, then, found Clive in the mood to test this question. Mír Jafar had thrown himself into his hands; he would use the chance to make it clear that he himself intended to be the real master, whilst prepared to render to the Súbahdár the respect and homage due to his position. Accordingly he started at once (November 17) for Murshidábád with all his available troops, now reduced at Calcutta to 400 English and 1300 sipáhís, and reached that place on the 25th, bringing with him the disaffected Rájá of Purniah. His peace he made with the Mír Jafar; then, joined by the 250 Europeans he had left at Kásimbázár, he proceeded to Rájmahál, and encamped there close to the army of the Súbahdár, who had marched it thither with the object of coercing Bihár.

This was Clive's opportunity. Bihár was very restive, and the Súbahdár could not coerce its nobles without the aid of the English. Clive declined to render that aid unless the Súbahdár should, before one of his soldiers marched, pay up all the arrears due to the English, and should execute every article of the treaty he had recently signed. For Mír Jafar the dilemma was terrible. He had not the money; he had made enemies by his endeavours to raise it. In this trouble he bethought him of Rájá Duláb Rám, recently his Finance Minister, but whom he had subsequently alienated. Through Clive's mediation a reconciliation was patched up with the Rájá. Then the matter was arranged in the manner Clive had intended it should be, by giving the English a further hold on the territories of the Súbahdár.

It was agreed that Clive should receive orders on the treasury of Murshidábád for twelve and a half lakhs of rupees; assignments on the revenues of Bardwán, Kishangarh, and Húglí for ten and a half: for the payments becoming due in the following April, assignments on the same districts for nineteen lakhs: then the cession of the lands south of Calcutta, so long deferred, was actually made—the annual rental being the sum of 222,958 rupees. These arrangements having been completed, Clive accompanied the Súbahdár to the capital of Bihár, the famous city of Patná. There they both remained, the Súbahdár awaiting the receipt of the imperial patents confirming him in his office; Clive resolved, whatever were the personal inconvenience to himself, not to quit Patná so long as the Súbahdár should remain there. They stayed there three months, a period which Clive utilized to the best advantage, as it seemed to him at the moment, of his countrymen. The province of Bihár was the seat of the saltpetre manufacture. It was a monopoly[9] farmed to agents, who re-sold the saltpetre on terms bringing very large profits. Clive proposed to the Súbahdár that the East India Company should become the farmers, and offered a higher sum than any at which the monopoly had been previously rated. Mír Jafar was too shrewd a man not to recognize the enormous advantages which must accrue to his foreign protectors by his acquiescence in a scheme which would place in their hands the most important trade in the country. But he felt the impossibility of resistance. He was a bird in the hands of the fowler, and he agreed.

[9] The possession of this monopoly became the cause of the troubles which followed the departure of Clive, and led to the life-and-death struggle with Mír Kásim.

At length (April 14) the looked-for patents arrived. Accompanying that which gave to the usurpation of Mír Jafar the imperial sanction was a patent for Clive, creating him a noble of the Mughal empire, with the rank and title of a Mansabdar[10] of 6000 horse. The investiture took place the day following. Then, after marching to Bárh, the two armies separated, the Súbahdár proceeding to Murshidábád; Clive, after a short stay at that place, to Calcutta.

[10] For the nature of Mansab, and the functions of the holder of a Mansab (or Mansabdar) the reader is referred to Blochmann's *Ain-i-Akbarí*. By the original regulations of Akbar, who founded the order, the Mansabdars ranked from the Dahbashi, often Commander-in-Chief, to the Doh Hazári, Commander of 10,000 horse, to the Mansabdars of 6000 downwards. Vide *Ain-i-Akbarí*(Blochmann's), p. 237 and onwards.

Clive had returned to Calcutta, May 24, absolute master of the situation. He had probed to the bottom the character of the Súbahdár, and had realized that so long as he himself should remain in India, and Mír Jafar on the *masnad*, the English need fear no attack. But, in the East, one man's life, especially life of a usurper, is never secure. In those days the risks he incurred were infinitely greater than they are now. Clive had noted the ill-disguised impatience of several of the powerful nobles, more especially that of Míran, the son, and of Mír Kásim, the son-in-law, of the Súbahdár. He had left, then, the greater part of his English soldiers at Kásimbázár, close to the native capital, to watch events, whilst he returned to Calcutta to trace there the plan of a fortress which would secure the English against attack.

The fort so traced, received the name of its predecessor, built by Job Charnock in the reign of King William III, and called after him, Fort William.

Nearly one month later, June 20, there arrived from England despatches, penned after learning the recapture of Calcutta, but before any knowledge of the events which had followed that recapture, ordering a new constitution for the administering of the Company's possessions in Bengal. The text of the constitution, ridiculous under any circumstances, was utterly unadapted to the turn events had taken. It nominated ten men, not one of whom was competent for the task, to administer the affairs of Bengal. The name of Clive was not included amongst the ten names. It was not even mentioned. Fortunately for the Company, the ten men nominated had a clearer idea of their own fitness than had their honourable masters. With one consent, they represented the true situation to the Court of Directors, and then, with the same unanimity, requested Clive to accept the office of President, and to exercise its functions, until the pleasure of the Court should be known. Clive could not but accede to their request.

For, indeed, it was no time for weak administration and divided counsels. Again had the French attempted to recover the position in Southern India which Clive had wrested from them. Count Lally, one of the brilliant victors of Fontenoy, had been sent to Pondicherry with a considerable force, and the news had just arrived that he was marching on Tanjore, having recalled Bussy and his troops from the court of the Súbahdár of the Deccan. With the news there had come also a request that the Government of Bengal would return to the sister Presidency the troops lent to her by the latter in the hour of the former's need to recover Calcutta.

Clive felt all the urgency of the request; the possible danger of refusing to comply with it; the full gravity of the situation at Madras. He also was one of those who had been lent. If the troops were to return, it was he who should lead them back. But he felt strongly that his place, and their place also, was in Bengal. Especially was it so in the presence of the rumours, already circulating, of great successes achieved by Lally, and by the French fleet. Such rumours, followed by his departure, would certainly incite the nobles of Bengal and Bihár, with or without Mír Jafar, to strike for the independence which they felt, one and all, he had wrested from them.

Matters, indeed, in the provinces of Bengal and Bihár had come to bear a very threatening aspect. The treasury of Mír Jafar was exhausted by his payments; his nobles were disaffected; the moneyed classes bitterly hostile. Threatened on his northern frontier by a rebellious son of the King of Delhi and by the Nawáb-Wazír of Oudh, Mír Jafar was in the state of mind which compels men of his stamp to have recourse to desperate remedies. For a moment he thought seriously of calling the Maráthás to his assistance. Then the conviction forced itself upon him that the remedy would be worse than the disease, and he renounced the idea. At last, when the army of the rebel prince had penetrated within Bihár, and was approaching Patná, he resigned himself to the inevitable, and besought abjectly the assistance of Clive.

Clive had resolved to help him when affairs in Southern India reached a point which required his immediate attention. A letter from the Rájá of Vizianagram reached him, informing him that the effect of the recall by Lally from Aurangábád of the troops under Bussy had been to leave the Northern Sirkárs[11] without sufficient protection; that he and other Rájás had risen in revolt, and urgently demanded the despatch thither of some English troops, by whose aid they could expel the few Frenchmen left there. It was characteristic of Clive to seize the points of a difficult situation. Few men who had to meet on their front a dangerous invasion, would have dared to despatch, to a distant point, the troops he had raised to repel that invasion, remaining himself to meet it from resources he would improvise. But, without a moment's hesitation or a solitary misgiving, Clive recognized that the opportunity had come to him to complete the work he had begun, six years before, in Southern India; that a chance presented itself to transfer the great influence exercised by Bussy at the court of the Súbahdár of the Deccan to his own nation. Leaving to himself then the care of Bengal and Bihár he directed a trusted officer, Colonel Forde, to proceed (October 12) with 500 Europeans, 2000 sipáhís, and some guns to Vizagapatam, to unite there with the Rájá's troops, to take command; and to expel the French from the Northern

Sirkárs: then, if it were possible, to assume at the court of the Súbahdár the influence which the French had till then exercised. It is only necessary here to say that Forde, who was one of the great Indian soldiers of the century, carried both points with skill and discretion. He beat the French in detail, and compelled them to yield their fortresses; and, when the Súbahdár marched to their aid, he succeeded, with rare tact, in inducing him to cede to the English the whole of the territories he had conquered, and to transfer the paramount influence at his court to the English. The victories of Forde laid the foundation of a predominance which, placed some forty years later on a definite basis by the great Marquess Wellesley, exists to the present day. It is not too much to assert that this splendid result was due to the unerring sagacity, the daring under difficult circumstances, of Robert Clive.

[11] The districts of Ganjám, Vizagapatam, Godávari, and Krishna.

Meanwhile the solicitations of Mír Jafar increased in importunity. Even the Great Mughal called upon Clive, as a Mansabdar, to assist him to repress the rebellion of his son. Clive did not refuse. As soon as his preparation had been completed, he set out, February, 1759, for Murshidábád with 450 Europeans and 2500 sipáhís, leaving the care of Calcutta to a few sick and invalids. He reached Murshidábád the 8th of March, and, accompanied by the Mír Jafar's army, entered Patná on the 8th of April. But the rumour of his march had been sufficient. Four days before the date mentioned the rebellious prince evacuated his positions before the city, and, eventually, sought refuge in Bundelkhand. Clive entered Patná in triumph; put down with a strong hand the disturbances in its vicinity; and then returned to Calcutta, in time enough to hear of the victorious course of Forde, although not of its more solid result.

Before he had quitted Patná, Mír Jafar had conferred upon him, as a personal jágír,[12] the Zamíndárí of the entire districts south of Calcutta then rented by the East India Company.

[12] A jágír is, literally, land given by a government as a reward for services rendered. A Zamíndárí, under the Mughal government, meant a tract, or tracts of land held immediately of the government on condition of paying the rent of it. By the deed given to Clive, the East India Company, which had agreed to pay the rents of those lands to the Súbahdár, would pay them to Clive to whom the Súbahdár had, by this deed, transferred his rights. It may here be added that the Company denied the right of Clive to the rents which amounted to £30,000 per annum, and great bitterness ensued. The matter was ultimately compromised.

Clive had scarcely returned to Calcutta when there ensued complications with the Dutch.

During the sixteenth and seventeenth centuries Holland had posed in the East as a rival, often a successful rival, of the three nations which had attempted to found settlements in those regions. She had established a monopoly of trade with the Moluccas, had possessed herself of several islands in the vicinity of the Straits, had expelled Portugal from Malacca (1641), from Ceylon (1658), from the Celebes (1663), and from the most important of her conquests on the coasts of Southern India (1665). In the beginning of the eighteenth century the Dutch-Indian Company possessed in the east seven administrations; four directorial posts; four military commands; and four factories. The Company was rich, and had but few debts.

Amongst the minor settlements it had made was the town of Chinsurah, on the Húglí, twenty miles above Calcutta. Chinsurah was a subordinate station, but, until the contests between the Nawáb and the English, it had been a profitable possession. We have seen how, under the pressure of Clive, Mír Jafar had made to the English some important trade-concessions. It was certain that sooner or later, these would affect the trade, the profits, and the self-respect, of the European rivals of Great Britain. Prominent as traders amongst these were the Dutch. Amongst the changes which they felt most bitterly were (1) the monopoly, granted to the English, of the saltpetre trade; (2) the right to search all vessels coming up the Húglí; (3) the employment of no other than English pilots. These injuries, as they considered them, rankled in their breasts, and they resolved to put a stop to them. To effect that purpose they entered into secret negotiations with Mír Jafar. These, after a time, ended in the entering into an agreement in virtue of which, whilst the Dutch covenanted to despatch to the Húglí a fleet and army sufficiently strong to expel the English from Bengal, the Súbahdár pledged himself to prepare with the greatest secrecy an army to co-operate with them. This agreement was signed in November, 1758, just after Clive had despatched Forde, with all the troops then available, to the Northern Sirkárs, but before his march to Patná, recorded, with its consequences, in the preceding pages. The secret had been well kept, for Clive had no suspicion of the plot. He knew he had the Súbahdár in the hollow of his hand, so far as related to the princes of the soil; he knew the French were powerless to aid the Súbahdár: and he never thought of the little settlement of Chinsurah.

In the month of June, 1759, just following the return of Clive to Calcutta, the Mír Jafar received from the Dutch a secret intimation that their plans were approaching maturity. He stayed then but a short time at the English seat of government, but returned thither in October, to be at hand when the expected crisis should occur. Meanwhile rumours had got about that a considerable Dutch fleet was approaching the Húglí, and, in fact, a large Dutch vessel, with Malayan soldiers, did arrive at Diamond Harbour. Clive had at once demanded from the Dutch authorities an explanation, at the same time that he innocently apprised Mír Jafar of the circumstance, and of the rumour. The Dutch authorities explained that the ship had been bound for Nágapatnam, but had been forced by stress of weather to seek refuge in the Húglí.

In October, whilst Mír Jafar was actually in Calcutta, the Dutch made their spring. It was a very serious attack, for the Dutch had four ships, carrying each thirty-six guns; two, each carrying twenty-six; one, carrying sixteen, and had on board these 700 European soldiers and 800 Malays: at Chinsurah they had 150 Europeans, and a fair number of native levies: behind them they had the Súbahdár. To meet them Clive had but three Indiamen, each carrying thirty guns, and a small despatch-boat. Of soldiers, he had, actually in Calcutta and the vicinity, 330 Europeans, and 1200 sipáhís. The nearest of the detachments in the country was too distant to reach the scene of action in time to take part in the impending struggle. There was aid, however, approaching, that he knew not of.

Clive revelled in danger. In its presence his splendid qualities shone forth with a brilliancy which has never been surpassed. His was the soul that animated the material figures around him. His the daring with which he could inspire his subordinates; imbue them with his own high courage; and make them, likewise, 'conquer the impossible.'

His conduct on the occasion I am describing is pre-eminently worthy of study. A short interview with Mír Jafar filled his mind with grave suspicions. He did not show them. He even permitted Mír Jafar to proceed to Húglí to have an interview with the Dutch authorities. But when the Súbahdár despatched to him from that place a letter in which he stated that he had simply granted to the Dutch some indulgences with respect to their trade, he drew the correct conclusion, and prepared to meet the double danger.

In his summary of the several courses he would have to adopt he dismissed altogether the Súbahdár from his mind. Him he feared not. With the Dutch he would deal and deal summarily. He had already despatched special messengers to summon every available man from the outposts. He now called out the militia, 300 men, five-sixths of whom were Europeans, to defend the town and fort; he formed half a troop of volunteer horsemen, and enlisted as volunteer infantry all the men who could not ride; he ordered the despatch-boat to sail with all speed to the Arakan coast, where she would find a squadron under Admiral Cornish ready to send him aid; he ordered up, to lie just below the fort, the three Indiamen of which I have spoken: he strengthened the two batteries commanding the most important passages of the river near Calcutta, and mounted guns on the nascent Fort William. Then, when he had completed all that 'Prudentia' could suggest, the rival goddess, 'Fortuna'[13] smiled upon him. Just as he was completing his preparations, Colonel Forde and Captain Knox, fresh from the conquest of the Northern Sirkárs, arrived to strengthen his hand. To the former Clive assigned the command of the whole of his available force in the field: to the latter, the charge of the two batteries.

[13] 'Nullum numen abest si sit Prudentia; nos te, Nos facimus Fortuna, deam.' *Juvenal.*

Up to that period the Dutch had endeavoured to pose as peaceful traders. But no sooner had their negotiations with Mír Jafar been completed, and they had received his permission to ascend to Chinsurah, than they threw off the mask, and sent an ultimatum to Clive threatening vengeance unless the English should renounce their claim of the right of search, and redress the other grievances they enumerated. Clive replied that in all his actions he had been guided by the authority vested in him by the Súbahdár, the representative of the Great Mughal; that he was powerless in the matter; but that if they would refer their complaints to the Súbahdár, he would gladly act the part of mediator. The Dutch commander, however, paid no heed to this somewhat vague reply, but acted as though it were a declaration of war. For, on receipt of Clive's letter he attacked and captured seven small vessels lying off Falta, among them the despatch-boat above referred to, tore down the English colours, and transferred the guns and material to their own ships. Then, having plundered the few houses on the riverbanks, he continued his upward course, with his ships, although, from the want of pilots, their progress was necessarily slow.

Clive, on hearing of these demonstrations, prepared to act on the instant. First, he sent a despatch to the Súbahdár, telling him that the quarrel between the two European nations must be fought out alone, adding, however, to test Mír Jafar, a paragraph to the effect that the Súbahdár would convince him of his sincerity and attachment if he would directly surround their (the Dutch) subordinates, and distress them in 'the country to the utmost.' Then he ordered Forde to occupy Bárnagar on the left bank of the Húglí, five miles from Calcutta; to cross thence with his troops and four field-pieces to Shirirámpur, nine miles distant; to be ready, either there or beyond it, to intercept the Dutch troops, in the event of their trying to reach Chinsurah by land. Then, learning that the Dutch ships had progressed as far as the Sankrál reach, just below the fire of the English batteries, and were landing their troops with directions to march directly on Chinsurah, he issued orders for immediate action.

Recognizing on the instant that, by landing, the enemy's troops had severed themselves from their base—the ships—he despatched Knox to join Forde, and sent information to the latter of the probable route the enemy's troops would take, leaving it to him to deal with them as he might consider advisable. Then he sent orders to Commodore Wilson, the senior of the captains of the Indiamen, to demand from the Commander of the Dutch squadron a full apology for the insults he and his subordinates had been guilty of, the return of the individuals and of the plunder he and they had taken, and their immediate departure from the Húglí. Failing prompt compliance with all these demands, Wilson was to attack the enemy's squadron.

The scene that followed deserves to rank with the most glorious achievements of English sailors. The three captains were all built in the heroic mould. Not one of them felt a doubt of victory when they were ordered to attack a squadron in all respects more than double in numbers and weight of metal to their own. It must suffice here to say[14] that, the proposal of the English Commodore having been refused by the Dutch, the English captains bore down upon the enemy; after a contest of little more than two hours, captured or sank six of their ships; the seventh, hurrying out to sea, fell into the hands of two ships of war, then entering the river. Well might the victors exclaim, in the language of our great national poet:—

        'O, such a
  day,
  So fought, so followed, and so fairly won,
  Came not till now to dignify the times,
  Since Caesar's fortunes.'

[14] For a detailed account of this action see the author's *Decisive Battles of India*.

This success left the Dutch soldiers, then on their way to Chinsurah, absolutely without a base. They could only find safety in success, and success was denied them. They were first repulsed by Forde in an attack they made on a position he had taken at Chandranagar, and the next day almost destroyed by the same gallant officer, joined by Knox, in a battle at the village of Biderra, nearly midway between Chandranagar and Chinsurah. Few victories have been more decisive. Of the 700 Europeans and 800 Malays landed from the ships, 120 of the former and 200 of the latter were left dead on the field; 300, in about equal proportions, were wounded; and the remainder, with the exception of 60 Dutch and 250 Malays, were taken prisoners. Forde had under his command on this eventful day (November 25) 320 Europeans, 800 sipáhís, and 50 European volunteer cavalry. The previous day, reckoning that he would have to fight the enemy with his inferior numbers, he had sent a note to Clive asking for implicit instructions. Clive, who was playing whist when the note reached him, knowing with whom he was dealing, wrote across it, in pencil: 'Dear Forde, Fight them immediately: I will send you the order in Council to-morrow,' and sent back the messenger with it.

The two victories were in all respects decisive. Never again did the Dutch trouble the tranquillity of India. Mír Jafar was cowed. Three days after the victory of Biderra, his son, Míran, arrived from Murshidábád with 6,000 horse, for the purpose, he explained, of exterminating the Dutch. Clive, always merciful in victory, gave to these, against their baffled confederate, the protection which he considered due to a foe no longer to be dreaded.

Clive now regarded the British position in Bengal so secure that he might return to England to enjoy there the repose and the position he had acquired. He had compressed into three years achievements the most momentous, the most marvellous, the most enduring, recorded in the history of his country. Landing with a small force below Calcutta in the last days of 1756, he had compelled the Súbahdár, who had been responsible for the Black Hole tragedy, though guiltless of designing it,[15] to evacuate Calcutta, to witness without interfering his capture of Chandranagar. Determined, then, in the interests of his country, to place matters in Bengal on such a footing that a repetition of the tragedy of 1756 should be impossible, he resolved to replace Siráj-ud-daulá, himself the son of a usurper, by a native chieftain who should owe everything to the English, and who would probably allow himself to be guided by them in his policy. To this end he formed a conspiracy among his nobles, fomented discontent among his people, and finally forced him to appeal to arms. At Plassey Clive risked everything on the fidelity to himself of the conspirators with whom he had allied himself. They were faithful. He gained the battle, not gloriously but decisively, and became from the morrow of the victory the lord paramount of the noble whom he placed then on the *masnad*. Possibly it was partly policy which impelled him to give his nominee no chance from the beginning. Certain it is, that Mír Jafar was, from the moment of his accession, so handicapped by the compulsion to make to his allies enormous payments, that his life, from that moment to the hour of his deposition, presently to be related, was not worth living. The commercial concessions which Clive had forced from him gave the English an *imperium in imperio*. But the Súbahdár was in the toils. When invasion came from the north he tried his utmost to avoid asking for the aid of Clive. But Clive, who had sent his best soldiers to conquer the Northern Sirkárs, and to establish permanent relations with the Súbahdár of the Deccan—relations which secured to England a permanent predominance in the most important districts of southern India—was indispensable. His assistance, given in a manner which could not fail to impress the natives of India—for the enemy fled at his approach—riveted the chains on the Súbahdár. Then came the invasion of the Dutch. For the first time a superior hostile force of Europeans landed on the shores of British India. The Súbahdár, anxious above all things to recover his freedom of action, promised them his assistance. Clive shone out here, more magnificently than he had shone before, as the undaunted hero. Disdaining to notice the action of the Súbahdár, he gave all his attention to the European invaders; with far inferior means he baffled their schemes; and crushed them in a manner such as would make them, and did make them, remember and repent the audacity which had allowed them to imagine that they could impose their will on the victor of Káveripák and Plassey. He had made the provinces he had conquered secure, if only the rule which was to follow his own should be based on justice, against the native rulers; secure for ever against European rivals assailing it from the sea.

[15] Siráj-ud-daulá had given instructions that the prisoners should be safely cared for, and had then gone to sleep. It was the brutality of his subordinate officers which caused the catastrophe.

That, during this period, he had committed faults, is only to say that he was human. But, unfortunately, some of his faults were so grave as to cast a lasting stain on a career in many respects worthy of the highest admiration. The forging of the name of Admiral Watson, although the name was attached to the deed with, it is believed, his approval,[16] was a crime light in comparison with the purpose for which it was done—the deceiving of the Bengálí, Aminchand. It is true that Aminchand was a scoundrel, a blackmailer, a man who had said: 'Pay me well, or I will betray your secrets.' But that was no reason why Clive should fight him with his own weapons: should descend to the arena of deceit in which the countrymen of Aminchand were past-masters. Possibly the atmosphere he breathed in such society was answerable, to a great extent, for this deviation from the path of honour. But the stain remains. No washing will remove it. It affected him whilst he still lived, and will never disappear.

[16] In his evidence before the Committee of the House of Commons Clive said regarding the fictitious treaty: 'It was sent to Admiral Watson, who objected to the signing of it; but, to the best of his remembrance, gave the gentleman who carried it (Mr. Lushington) leave to sign his name upon it.'

Then again, as to his dealings with Siráj-ud-daulá and Mír Jafar. The whole proceedings of Clive after his capture of Calcutta prove that he intended to direct all his policy to the removal of that young prince from the *masnad*. Some have thought that the Black Hole tragedy was the cause of this resolve. But this can hardly be so, for Mír Jafar, the commander-in-chief of the army which seized Calcutta in 1756, was equally implicated in that transaction. The suggestion that Siráj-ud-daulá was intriguing with the French at Haidarábád is equally untenable, for Clive knew he had little cause to fear their hostility. Clive not only expelled that prince, but, by his policy, his extortions, his insistance to obtain control of the saltpetre traffic, rendered it impossible for his successor to govern. Success attended his policy so long as he remained on the spot to control his subordinates, but it was inevitable that, sooner or later, there would come a revulsion. The warlike natives of Bihár had not been conquered, and they knew it. They had helped Clive, not that they should become subject to the foreigner from the sea, but that they might have a native ruler whom they trusted, in place of one whom they disliked. When they realized that the result of this change was not only subjection to the islanders, but impoverishment to themselves, they broke into what was called rebellion, and showed on many a bloody field that it was not they, only Siráj-ud-daulá, who had been conquered at Plassey.

This was the most dangerous legacy of the policy and action of Clive. He recognized its shadowy existence. He wrote to his successor, Mr. Vansittart, when he transferred to him his own office, that the only danger he had to dread in Bengal was that which might arise from venality and corruption. He might have added that the spoils of Plassey had created a state of society in which those vices were prominent; that the saltpetre monopoly, with the duties and exemptions which had followed its acquisition, had confirmed them. The Súbahdár himself recognized the new danger which would follow the departure of Clive. In his mind he was the moderator who, satisfied himself, would have stayed the hands of others. To quiet the newcomers there would be fresh rapacity, more stringent despoilings. He felt, to use the expression of the period when Clive quitted Bengal, that 'the soul was departing from the body.'

Clive made over charge to Mr. Holwell, of Black Hole notoriety, pending the arrival of Mr. Vansittart, the 15th of February, 1760. With the sanction of the Court he had nominated Major Calliaud to be Commander of the Forces. Four members of his Council retired about the same time as himself.

CHAPTER XI
THE SECOND VISIT OF CLIVE TO ENGLAND

During his administration of four years in Bengal Clive had been greatly hampered by the contradictory orders he had received from the Court of Directors. In that Court there were four parties: the party of alarmists at the aggrandizement of the Company's possessions in India; the party of progressists; the middle party, composed of men who would retain all that had been conquered, but who, not understanding the necessity which often compels a conqueror to advance that he may retain, would on no account sanction the proceeding of a step further; a fourth party bent only on acquiring plunder. As one or other of these parties obtained preponderance in the Court, so did the orders transmitted to India take their colour. In those days, it must be remembered, there was no Board of Control to regulate and, if necessary, to modify, even entirely to alter, the rulings of the General Court. Thus it was that the agent on the spot, finding the orders from England constantly changing, was driven to rely upon his own judgement, and to act on his own responsibility. This did not signify so much so long as there was, on the spot, holding supreme authority, a Clive or a Warren Hastings. But when the local chief authority was in the hands of men wanting alike in intellect, in high principle, and in nerve, the situation was likely to become dangerous in the extreme.

For the moment, when Clive quitted India, the situation was tranquil. But it might become at any moment the reverse. Therefore it was that Clive had recommended as his successor a man whom he believed he had sounded to the core, and in whom he had found one after his own heart. But there is no proverb more true than that contained in the criticism passed by Tacitus on Galba, 'Omnium consensu capax imperii, nisi imperasset.' We shall see presently how the conduct of Vansittart corresponded to this aphorism.

A little more than a year before quitting the shores of Bengal, Clive had addressed to Mr. Pitt, afterwards Lord Chatham, then Secretary of State, a letter (January 7, 1759) in which he had represented the difficulties of the actual situation, and had suggested a mode of dealing with them. He had described the actual Súbahdár as a man attached to the English, and as likely to continue that attachment 'while he has no other support,' but totally uninfluenced by feelings of gratitude, feelings not common to his race. On the other hand, he was advanced in years; his son, Míran, was utterly unworthy, so unworthy 'that it will be almost unsafe trusting him with the succession.' He added immediately, as though prescient of the events which were to follow, 'In case of their,' the native princes, 'daring to be troublesome,' they—a body of 2000 English soldiers—would 'enable the Company to take the sovereignty upon themselves.' After detailing how the transfer would be easy, and palatable, rather than otherwise, to the natives generally, Clive proceeded to represent that so large a sovereignty might possibly be an object too extensive for a mercantile company, and to suggest that it might be worthy of consideration whether the Crown should not take the matter in hand. The points he urged were the following: First, the ease with which the English 'could take absolute possession of these rich kingdoms, and that with the Mughal's own consent, on condition of paying him less than a fifth of the revenues thereof.' There would remain a surplus of two millions, besides most valuable productions of nature and art. He dwelt, secondly, on the influence in Europe which would thereby accrue to England, and the enormous increase of prestige and of the advantages which prestige conveys, on the spot. He added that a small force of European troops would be sufficient, as he could enlist any number of sipáhís, who 'will very readily enter our service.' This letter he transmitted by the hands of Mr. Walsh, his secretary during the campaign of Plassey and the year following, and whom he describes as 'a thorough master of the subject,' 'able to explain to you the whole design and the facility with which it may be executed.'

Mr. Pitt received the letter, but was deterred from acting upon it by difficulties which arose in his mind from his want of knowledge of India and of matters connected with that country. To the son of a man whose father had been Governor of Madras in the days when the English were the humble lessees of the lords of the soil, the proposition to become masters of territories far larger and richer than their island home, seemed beset with difficulties which, if it may be said without disrespect to his illustrious memory, existed solely in his own imagination—for they have since been very easily overcome.

The letter served to make Clive personally known to the great statesman when he landed in England in September or October, 1760. He had returned a very rich man; he was full of ambition; his fame as a soldier had spread all over the kingdom. Pitt, shortly before his arrival (1758), had spoken of him in the House of Commons as a 'Heaven-born General,' as the only officer, by land or sea, who had sustained the reputation of the country and added to its glory. The King himself, George II, when the Commander-in-chief had proposed to him to send the young Lord Dunmore to learn the art of war under Prince Ferdinand of Brunswick, had replied, 'What can he get by attending the Duke of Brunswick? If he want to learn the art of war, let him go to Clive.' These expressions show at least the temper of the times, the feelings which would inspire the welcome which England would give to her latest hero. And yet the welcome itself fell far short of that which Clive had anticipated. From the Crown there was no immediate recognition; from the Court of Directors, a hostile section of which held the supremacy, he received worse than neglect. Almost their first act was to dispute his right to the jágír which Mír Jafar had bestowed upon him.[1] From the general public there was no demonstration. Clive felt that in England as in India he would have to fight his way upwards.

[1] See Chapter X.

His health was not very good. He suffered from rheumatism, which had assailed him in Bengal, and which bore a strong resemblance to rheumatic gout. Scarcely had he recovered from this malady when he was assailed by the insidious disease which, afterwards, but rarely left him. This caused a depression of spirits which gradually wore out his body. As a boy he had suffered at intervals from similar attacks. They increased now in intensity, baffling the physicians who attended him. He bore up bravely, however, and pushed forward with his wonted energy the ambitious plans he had formed in the intervals of quiet and repose.

At the age of thirty-five, with an enormous fortune, great ambition, and sanguine hopes for the future, Clive trusted that the illness he suffered from would eventually yield to treatment, and he entered on his campaign in England with the confidence in himself which had been one secret of his success in India. He had hoped, on his arrival, to have been at once raised to the House of Peers. But the honours of the Crown, long delayed, took the shape only of an Irish peerage. With this he was forced to be content, and, being debarred from the Upper House, made all his arrangements to become a member of the Lower. He speedily obtained a seat in that House.

Possibly he marred his prospects by the line which he took in politics. In October, 1760, George II had died. The new King, whose proudest boast was that he had been born an Englishman, made Lord Bute Secretary of State. Soon after Pitt resigned, because the rest of the Ministry refused to support him in his policy of going to war with Spain, the Duke of Newcastle still remaining nominal head of the Cabinet. In 1762 the Duke resigned, and Lord Bute became Prime Minister. Sir John Malcolm states that Lord Clive was offered his own terms if he would support the Bute Ministry. But Clive had given his mental adhesion in another quarter, and therefore refused his support, and was, it is stated, treated coldly in consequence.[2]

[2] Vide Malcolm's *Clive*, vol. ii. p. 203: also Gleig, p. 134. There would seem to be some mistake as to the reason given by Mr. Gleig for his statement that Clive refused his support to the Bute Administration because of his devotion to George Grenville; for George Grenville held the post of one of the principal Secretaries of State in Lord Bute's Ministry.

Though not a supporter of the Bute Administration, Clive did not refrain from volunteering to it his advice when the preliminaries of peace between France and England were under discussion. Both Powers were resolved that the peace should extend to their possessions in India. Clive wrote therefore to Lord Bute suggesting the terms upon which, in his opinion, it was absolutely necessary for the safety of the East India Company he should insist. Prominent among these were (1) the absolute limitation of the number of troops the French might retain in Southern India, and (2) a prohibition to admit into Bengal Frenchmen other than those engaged in commercial enterprises. Lord Bute so far followed the advice as to induce the French to agree not to maintain troops either in Bengal or the Northern Sirkárs. But when he would go further, and, on the suggestion of Mr. Lawrence Sulivan, Chairman of the Court of Directors, make the recognition of certain native princes a clause in the projected treaty between the two Powers, Clive, with his habitual prescience, denounced the clause as fraught with consequences most disastrous to the position of England in India, and persuaded the Minister to withdraw it.

The gentleman above referred to, Mr. Lawrence Sulivan, had become, from pure motives of jealousy, one of the bitterest enemies of Clive. Sulivan had served in India without distinction, but had succeeded in amassing there a handsome fortune, and being a man of bold address and pushing manners, had become a Director of the Company. Whilst Clive was still in India Sulivan had professed the most unbounded admiration for him and his achievements, and, by thus professing, had obtained the support of the followers of Clive when he made a bid for the Chairmanship of the Court. This he secured, and, being a man of considerable self-assertion and determination, succeeded in becoming the dictator of the Council. Up to that time he had given his support to Clive, but no sooner did he hear of the departure of his hero for England, than, dreading the effect of his arrival upon his own influence, he had become his most bitter opponent. He it was who stimulated his colleagues to object to the donation of the jágír to Clive, mentioned in a previous page. The grounds to the objection were rather hinted at than expressed, for in those days the Court could not deny the right of the Súbahdár to bestow, or of Clive to accept, so handsome a gift. The real motive was to exclude Clive from a seat in the India House, and for a time Sulivan succeeded.

The hostility of Sulivan found an outcome in the progress of political affairs. Clive had voted against the Peace of Paris (February 10, 1763). Lord Bute, indignant at the opposition his measure encountered, had made his power felt by dismissing three dukes from their lord-lieutenancies, and he was very angry with Clive. He then sought and obtained the alliance of Sulivan to crush him. Up to that point Clive had remained quiescent; but at this new outrage he turned. Very shortly afterwards Sulivan came before the Court of Proprietors for re-election. To defeat him Clive had purchased a large amount of India Stock and divided it amongst his friends. At the show of hands there was a large majority against Sulivan, but when the ballot-box was appealed to the position was reversed, and Sulivan and his majority were returned.For the moment Clive's defeat was crushing, and he prepared to meet the consequences of it. His opponents did not delay to show their hands. Again was the question of the jágír mooted. The eminent counsel employed by Clive gave an opinion that the Court had no case. However, the Sulivan party persevered. Just on the eve of the trial, however, there came news from India which produced a revolution of opinion in the Court. The reports from Calcutta showed that the combined avarice, greed, misgovernment, and tyranny of the civil authorities left by Clive in Calcutta had produced a general uprising; had almost undone the great work Clive had accomplished; that there was no one on the spot who could be trusted to restore order; but that unless such a task were committed to a competent man, the possessions of the Company in Bengal would be in the greatest danger. This intelligence caused a panic in the India House. Instinctively the name of Clive came uppermost to every lip. The Proprietors were summoned to meet in full Court. Panic-stricken, they forced upon Clive the office, not merely of President, but of Governor-General, with very full powers. That their conduct regarding the jágír might not be pleaded by him as an objection to accept office, the Proprietors passed a resolution that the proceedings regarding the jágír should be stopped, and that the right of Clive to it should be officially recognized.

This was indeed a triumph. The policy, *reculer pour mieux sauter*, had been eminently justified. But Clive was as generous in victory as he had been great in defeat. He declined to profit by the enthusiasm of the Proprietors. Declaring that he had a proposal to make regarding the jágír, which he was confident the Court would accept, he proceeded to declare that it would be impossible for him to proceed to India leaving behind him a hostile Court and a hostile chairman; that at least the existing chairman must be changed. He carried the Proprietors with him, and measures were taken for a fresh election.

This election took place on the 25th of April, 1764. At it one-half of the candidates proposed by Sulivan were defeated, he himself being returned by a majority of one only. The chairman and deputy-chairman elected were both supporters of Clive. In the interval (March, 1764) Clive had been nominated Governor-General and Commander-in-chief of Bengal. To draw the fangs of the Council in Calcutta, four gentlemen were nominated to form with him a Select Committee authorized to act on their own authority, without reference to the Council.

One word, before the great man returns to the scenes of his triumphs, clothed with the fullest authority, regarding the instrument used by Mr. Sulivan and his friends to torture him. No sooner had the new Court been elected than Clive made to it his suggestion regarding the jágír. He proposed, and the Court agreed, that for a period of ten years, the company should pay to him the full amount of the jágír rents, unless he should die before, when the payments would cease; the ultimate disposal of the jágír to be made when the occasion should arise.

These matters having been settled, the officers to serve under him having been selected by himself, Clive, attended by two of the four members who had been appointed by the Court to accompany him, Messrs. Sumner and Sykes, embarked for Calcutta the 4th of June, 1764. Lady Clive did not go with him. She had to remain in England to superintend the education of her children.

CHAPTER XII
THE REIGN OF MISRULE IN BENGAL

Clive had chosen Mr. Vansittart to succeed him as President of the Council in Bengal because he believed he had recognized in him a man who would do all in his power to put down the growing system of venality and corruption. I have already shown how he had written to him before he quitted India. The words he had used were: 'The expected reinforcements will, in my opinion, put Bengal out of all danger but that of venality and corruption.' But Clive had not sufficiently considered that the very fact that the new President had been selected from Madras instead of from amongst the men who had served under his immediate orders was likely to cause jealousy among the latter; that Vansittart, notwithstanding his estimated lofty moral nature,[1] had no strength of character; no such persuasive powers as could win men to his side; no pre-eminent abilities; no force of will, such as Clive himself would have displayed, to dominate or, in case of great emergency, to suspend a refractory colleague. He was but one of the herd, well-meaning, opposed in principle to the venality and corruption then in vogue, but, in every sense of the term, ordinary. Even with respect to the two vices he denounced, he was an untried and untempted man.

[1] One anecdote will demonstrate the extent of the 'lofty moral nature' attributed by Clive to Mr. Vansittart. After Clive had been a year or so in England he wrote to Vansittart requesting him to select for him and despatch to him an elephant, as he wished to present one to the King. Vansittart chose and despatched the elephant for presentation to his Majesty, not as a gift from Clive, but as from himself.

His capacity for rule was put to the test very soon after he had assumed the reins of office. Those reins had not, as I have said, been handed to him by Clive. He had taken them from Mr. Holwell at the very end of July (1760). In the interval an event had occurred which had changed the general position in Bengal. Five months after Clive had quitted Calcutta (July 2, 1760) Míran, the only son of the Súbahdár, Mír Jafar, was struck dead by lightning. The reader may recollect the passage in his letter to Mr. Pitt, wherein Clive referred to this young man. He had described him as 'so cruel, worthless a young fellow, and so apparently an enemy to the English, that it will be almost unsafe trusting him with the succession.' If another successor, with an unquestionable title, had been immediately available, the death of Míran would have been no calamity. But there was no such successor. The next son in order of succession had seen but thirteen summers. Outside of that boy and his younger brothers were many claimants, not one of them with an indefeasible title. Mír Jafar himself was older even than his years. It devolved then, with the tacit consent of the nobles, on the Council at Calcutta, to nominate the successor to Míran. Such was the state of affairs when Mr. Vansittart arrived, and took his seat as President of the Council.

It happened that there were in Bengal at this time two officers who had rendered conspicuous service to the State, Majors Calliaud and Knox. During the very month in which Clive had quitted Calcutta, these officers had marched with such English troops and sipáhís as were available, to assist in the repelling of an invasion made by the titular King of Delhi, prompted, it was believed, by Míran, and had repulsed, with great loss to the enemy, an attempt made to storm the city of Patná. Vansittart, who knew Calliaud well alike as a friend and as a man trusted by Clive, summoned him to attend the Council upon the deliberations of which the future of Bengal depended. The discussions were long and somewhat heated. The party in the Council which represented most accurately the opinions of Clive, as rendered in his letter to Mr. Pitt, already referred to,[2] was of opinion that whilst Mír Jafar should be allowed to reign during the remainder of his life, opportunity should be taken of his death to transfer the directadministration to the English. If this opportunity had been taken to carry out some such policy it is probable that the evils which followed would have been avoided.

[2] Clive's letter had been written during the life of Míran. After detailing his character and the growing infirmities of Mír Jafar, he had added: 'so small a body as 2000 Europeans will secure us against any apprehensions from either the one or the other; and, in case of their daring to be troublesome, enable the Company to take the sovereignty upon themselves.'

The discussions were still proceeding when there arrived an envoy from the Súbahdár, his son-in-law, Mír Muhammad Kásim, a man of ability, tact, great persuasive powers, no scruple, and, in a certain sense, a patriot. Mír Kásim had coveted the succession vacant by the death of Míran. He had divined the plans of the English; he hated them as the enemies of the race of conquerors who had ruled Bengal and its people for centuries. He despised them as venal: and he had resolved to use them for his own advantage. He had brought with him a bag full of promises, and, though nominally the representative of Mír Jafar, had come resolved to work for his own interests.

Admitted into the secret deliberations of the Council, Mír Kásim soon realized that, with the single exception of Major Calliaud, he could buy them all. Even the scrupulousness of Mr. Vansittart vanished before his golden arguments. He bought them. For certain specified sums of money to be paid by him to each member of Council,[3] these official Englishmen covenanted to dethrone their ally of Plassey, Mír Jafar, and to seat on the *masnad* his son-in-law, Mír Kásim. Three days after the signature of the treaty Mír Kásim set out to make his preparations for the coming event, and two days afterwards Mr. Vansittart started for Murshidábád to break the news to Mír Jafar. His very first official act had been a violation of the principle prescribed to him by Clive as the one the non-indulgence in which would secure the English from all danger.

[3] He included even Major Calliaud, but without the consent, and after the departure from India, of that officer.

The events which followed must be stated very briefly. Vansittart obtained from Mír Jafar his resignation. The one condition stipulated by the old man was that thenceforth he should reside, under the protection of the English, at Calcutta, or in its immediate vicinity. For that city he started the following morning (September 19). Mír Kásim proceeded to Patná to complete the arrangements which had followed the repulse of the invasion of Bihár by the troops of Sháh Alím, and was there formally installed by Sháh Alím himself as Súbahdár of Bengal, Bihár, and Orissa.

Mír Kásim possessed all the capacities of a ruler. He knew thoroughly the evils under which the three provinces were groaning, and he proceeded with all the energy of a nature which never tired to reform them. He moved his capital to Mungír, a town with a fortress, on the right bank of the Ganges, commanding Northern and Eastern Bihár, and nearly midway between Calcutta and Benares. He then proceeded to reform his infantry on the English system, enlisting in his service two well-known soldiers of mixed or Armenian descent, Samru andMarkar, to command brigades of their own, and to aid in the training of the other soldiers. So far he achieved success. But when he proceeded to alleviate the misery of his people, he found that the fatal gift of the salt monopoly enabled the English to thwart all his efforts. For not only did the English use the authority they possessed to the great impoverishment of the soil, but they gave to their friends and dependents licences exempting from the payment of duty in such profusion, that the people of Bengal and Bihár suffered to an extent such as, in the present day, can with difficulty be credited. Never, on the one side, was there so insatiable a determination to become rich, no matter what misery might be thereby caused to others; never, on the other, a more honest endeavour, by sacrifices of any kind, to escape the ruin caused by such cruel exactions.

At last, when he had exhausted appeal after appeal to the Calcutta authorities, Mír Kásim recognized that his only chance of escape from the pressure too hard to be borne, was to appeal to the God of Battles. He was ready; the English, he believed, were not. He had excellent fighting material; generals who would not betray him. On the other hand, he knew that Clive and Calliaud had quitted India, and he did not believe that either had his equal amongst the men on the spot. Accordingly, just after he had received a demand from Calcutta, compliance with which would have completed the ruin then impending, he took the bold step of abolishing all transit duties, and of establishing free-trade throughout his territories. Anticipating the consequences of this bold act, he notified to his generals to be prepared for any movement the English might make.

Here, in the space allotted,[4] it must suffice to state that the English, amazed that such a worm as the Súbahdár of the three provinces should dare to question their commands, sent two of their number to remonstrate with him. But, whilst they were negotiating, another Englishman, one of their own clique, a civil officer named Ellis, furious at the idea of stooping to negotiate, made preparations to seize the important city of Patná. At the head of a small force he did surprise (June 25, 1763) that city during the hours before daybreak, but the garrison of the citadel and of a large stone building refused to admit him. Little caring for this, he permitted his men to disperse to plunder. Meanwhile the commander of the Súbahdár's troops, Mír Mehdí Khán, had started for Mungír to represent to his master the turn events had taken. On his way thither, a few miles from the city, he encountered the troops in his master's service commanded by Markar, the Armenian. Markar, as in duty bound, at once marched on Patná, found the English still plundering, drove them out of the city, and forced them to take refuge in a factory outside of it. There he besieged them, and thence he forced them to retreat (June 29). Meanwhile the Súbahdár had despatched his other brigade, under Samru, to Baksar, to cut off the retreat of the English, whilst he urged Markar to follow them up. Markar followed, caught, and attacked them between the two places—the 1st of July—and completely defeated them. The English, of whom there were 300, aided by 2,500 natives, fought with their usual courage; but they were badly led, were discouraged, and were completely beaten. Those who did not fall on the field were taken prisoners, re-conveyed to Patná, and were there eventually put to death.

[4] For a detailed account of the events preceding and following this action on the part of Mír Kásim, the reader is referred to the author's *Decisive Battles of India*, New Edition, pp. 133-174.

Such was the mode in which the war began. Had not the English possessed, though they knew it not until experience had taught them, a commander not inferior to any of the men who had done so much for the glory of their country in the East, it is probable that Mír Kásim, who, according to a contemporary writer,[5] 'was trained to arms,' and who 'united the gallantry of the soldier with the sagacity of the statesman,' would have driven them to their ships.

[5] The author of an admirable book, written at the time, entitled *Transactions in India from 1756 to 1783*.

From such a fate they were saved by the skill, the devotion, the supreme military talents of Major John Adams. This officer, placed in command, defeated Mír Kásim's army, after a very bloody battle, at Kátwá (July 19); again, a few days later, after a most stubborn resistance, at Gheriá. But neither of these battles was decisive of the war. When, however, the month following, Adams stormed the immensely strong position of Undwá Nala, defended by 40,000 men, and captured 100 pieces of cannon, Mír Kásim recognized that the war was over. He made no attempt to defend either Rájmahál, Mungír, or Patná. On the fall of the latter city (November 6) he fled to Oudh to take refuge there with the Nawáb-Wazír, and to instigate him to espouse his cause.

It is only necessary to add that he succeeded in persuading that prince to attempt the venture. He attempted it, however, only to repent his audacity, for, after much manoeuvring, the English, led by Munro, afterwards Sir Hector—who, after an interval of the incapable Carnac, had succeeded Adams, killed by the climate and the fatigues of the campaign—inflicted a crushing defeat upon him on the plains of Baksar (October 23, 1764); then Munro, pursuing his victorious course, occupied successively Benares, Chanár, and Allahábád. In March, 1765, the English overran Oudh, occupying Lucknow and Faizábád; then went on to beat the enemy at Karra, and again at Kálpi on the Jumna. Then the Nawáb-Wazír, 'a hopeless wanderer,' threw himself on the mercy of the conquerors. These behaved to him with conspicuous generosity, repaid by his successors in late years. The English frontier was, however, not the less advanced, practically, as far as Allahábád. Such was the military position when Clive returned to Calcutta as Governor in May, 1765.

Meanwhile the English, on the outbreak of the war with Mír Kásim, had restored Mír Jafar, receiving the usual gratuities for themselves and stipulating for exemptions from all duties except two and a half per cent. on salt. As for Mír Kásim, it is only necessary to add that he died some years later at Delhi in extreme poverty. With all his faults he was a patriot.

CHAPTER XIII
THE PURIFYING OF BENGAL

When Clive quitted England for Bengal (June 4, 1764) he knew only that the war with Mír Kásim was raging, and that Mír Jafar had been reinstated in his position. It was not until he reached Madras, the 10th of April following, that he learned that Mír Kásim had been finally defeated, that his followers had submitted, that Mír Jafar was dead, and that the Nawáb-Wazír of Oudh had thrown himself on the clemency of the English. In the interval of twenty-three days which elapsed before his arrival in Calcutta (May 3), he had time, in consultation with the two members of the Select Committee who accompanied him, Messrs. Sykes and Sumner, to deliberate regarding the course of action which it would behove him to adopt on his arrival there.[1]

[1] The other two were General Carnac and Mr. Verelst.

One of his first acts on arrival was to remodel the army. He placed General Carnac at its head, divided the European infantry into three battalions, gave regimental commands to two officers who had accompanied him from England, and regulated all the superior appointments in a manner the best adapted, in his opinion, to secure efficiency.

He dealt likewise with the Civil Service. Nothing had impressed Clive more than the evil effects of the predominance of venality and corruption during the rule which had followed his first departure, and he was resolved to put them down with a strong hand. He found, on his landing, a subject which gave him the opportunity he desired for showing publicly the bent of the line of conduct he intended to pursue.

Four months before his return, Mír Jafar, worn out by anxiety and trouble, had passed away. His position had become degraded, even in his own eyes. From having been, as he was on the morrow of Plassey, the lord of three rich provinces, he had become, to use the words of a contemporary Englishman,[2] 'a banker for the Company's servants, who could draw upon him as often and to as great an amount as they pleased.'

[2] Mr. Scrafton. See Scrafton's *Letters*.

We have seen how the members of Council had benefited pecuniarily by the elevation of Mír Jafar to the *masnad* in 1757; by that of his successor in 1763; by Mír Jafar's re-elevation the same year. The opportunity of again selecting a successor was not to be passed over without their once again plunging their hands in the treasury of Murshidábád. They found that there were two candidates for the vacant office, the son of Míran, and therefore grandson of Mír Jafar, and the eldest surviving son of that Nawáb. The decision arrived at by the Council, then reduced by vacancies to eight members, was to sell the succession to the candidate who should bid the highest price for it. They decided in favour of the son of Mír Jafar, for, although illegitimate, he was of an age at which he could act on his own authority; the other was a minor, whose revenues would have to be accounted for. In return for their complaisance, it was agreed that they should receive a sum of money, to be divided as they might arrange, close upon ten lakhs of rupees; in addition, there was to be paid another sum, just over ten lakhs, for secret services rendered by one of their number, Mr. Gideon Johnstone, and by a Muhammadan, Muhammad Ríza Khán, who also, in pursuance of the arrangement, was nominated Deputy-Nawáb. This shameful bargain was signed, sealed, and delivered on the 25th of February, little more than two months before Lord Clive landed.

An order from the India Office, which reached Calcutta just thirteen days before the death of Mír Jafar, and which prohibited—by a new covenant, to be signed by all the Civil Servants in India—the acceptance by such servants of presents of any kind from the natives of India, greatly strengthened the hands of Clive in dealing with this transaction. Finding that in the Council itself he would be subjected to much cavilling, he at once superseded its action by declaring (May 7) that the Select Committee[3] had been constituted. He then, with that Committee, assumed the whole powers of the Government, took an oath of secrecy, and had a similar oath administered to the only two of his colleagues who were present. He then set himself to examine all the matters connected with the succession to the office of Súbahdár of the three provinces.

[3] See Chapter XI.

He had to deal with men whom a long course of corruption had rendered absolutely shameless. Charged by Clive with having violated the orders of their masters in accepting presents after such acceptance had been prohibited, they replied that they had taken Clive himself as their model, and referred to his dealings with Mír Jafar in 1757, and afterwards at Patná, when he accepted the famous jágír. The reply naturally was that such presents were then permitted, whereas now they were forbidden. Clive added, among other reasoning, that then there was a terrible crisis; that for the English and Mír Jafar it was then victory or destruction, whereas now there was no crisis; the times were peaceful, the succession required no interference. He again charged the members of Council with having put up the Súbahdár for sale to the highest bidder, in order that they might put the price of it into their own pockets, and with having used indecent haste to complete the transaction before his arrival.

Clive could at the moment do no more than expose these men, now practically powerless. He forced them, however, to sign the new covenants. But his treatment of them rankled in their minds. They became his bitterest enemies, and from that time forward used all the means at their disposal to harass, annoy, and thwart him. When, finally, he drove them from the seats they had disgraced, in the manner presently to be related, they carried their bitterness, their reckless audacity, and their slanderous tongues to England, there to vent their spleen on the great founder of British India.

Having silenced these corrupt men, Clive turned his attention to the best means of regulating, on fair terms, commercial interests between the native and the foreigner. He soon recognized that the task of Hercules when he was set to cleanse the stables of King Augeas was light in comparison with the task he had undertaken. In the first place he was greatly hampered by the permission which the Court of Directors had granted to their Civil Servants to engage in private trade. So poorly paid were they, indeed, that private trade, or a compensation for it, had become necessary to them to enable them to live decently. The proposed compensation was afterwards adopted of fixing their salaries on a scale which would take away all temptation to indulge in other methods of obtaining money. Vainly did Clive press upon the Court the adoption of this alternative. Amongst our countrymen there is one class whose business it is to rule; but there are often other classes which aspire to that privilege, and which seize the opportunity afforded them to exercise power, but whose members possess neither the education, the enlightenment, nor the turn of mind to do so with success. Of this latter class were the men who had become the Directors of the East India Company. These men possessed no prescience; they were quite unable to make a correct forecast; they could consider only the present, and that dimly. They could not realize that the world was not standing still, and they would have denounced that man as a madman who should have told them that the splendid daring of Clive had made them the inheritors of the Mughal empire. Seeing only as far as the tips of their noses, these men declined to increase the salaries of their servants or to prohibit private trade.

Hercules could bend to his process of cleansing the stables of the King of Elis, the rivers Alpheus and Peneus. Clive could not bend the Court of Directors. The consequence was that his labour was great, his success incomplete. The utmost he could do, and did do, was to issue an order abrogating the privilege, used by the Civil Servants to the ruin of the children of the soil, to grant passes for the transit of merchandize free of duty; restricting such privilege to certain authorities named and defined. Upon the private trade of the civilians he imposed restrictions which minimized as far as was possible, short of its abolition, the evils resulting from permission to trade, bringing it in fact to a great extent under the control of the Government. In both these respects his reforms were wider, and went deeper, than those which Mír Kásim had vainly asked from Mr. Vansittart and his Council.

With regard to the salt monopoly, Clive had made investigations which proved that the trade in that commodity had been conducted in a manner which, whilst securing enormous profits for the few, had pressed very hardly on the many. He endeavoured to reduce this evil by placing the trade on a settled basis which, whilst it would secure to the natives a supply of the article at a rate not in excess of that which the poor man could afford, would secure to the servants of the Company fixed incomes on a graduated scale. His scheme, he knew, was far from being perfect, but it was the best he could devise in the face of the refusal of the India Office to increase salaries, and certainly it was a vast improvement on the system it superseded. Whilst it secured to the Company's servants in all departments an adequate, even a handsome, income, it reduced the price of salt to the natives to an amount from ten to fifteen per cent. below the average price to them of the preceding twenty years.

This accomplished, Clive proceeded to reconstitute the Calcutta Council. According to the latest orders then in existence this Council was composed of a president and sixteen members: but the fact of a man being a member of Council did not prevent him from accepting an agency in other parts of the Company's territories. The result was that many of the members held at the same time executive and supervising offices. They controlled, as councillors, the actions which they had performed as agents. There had been in consequence great laxity, much wrongdoing, complete failure of justice. Clive remedied this evil by ruling that a member of Council should be that and nothing more. He encountered great opposition, even amongst the members of the Select Committee, but he carried through his scheme.

Of this Select Committee it may here be stated that Clive used its members solely as a consultative committee. Those members had their duties, not always in Calcutta. Thus, whilst Carnac was with the army, Sykes acted at Murshidábád as the Governor's agent; Verelst supervised the districts of Burdwán and Mednípur. Mr. Sumner alone remained with Clive. This gentleman had been nominated to succeed Clive in case of his death or resignation. But it had become evident to Clive long before the period at which we have arrived that he was in every way unfitted for such an office. Infirm of purpose, sympathizing to a great extent with the corrupt party, wanting in energy, Sumner had given Clive but a slack support. This was the case especially in the matter of the reform of the Council just narrated.

Pursuing his inquiries Clive soon discovered that the administration of the civil districts and divisions by the Company's officers had been as faulty and corrupt as it well could be. The case, after examination and report, was tersely put by the Court of Directors in their summary of the state of Bengal on his arrival there. They described the three provinces, Bengal, Bihár, and Orissa, as 'a *súbah*'[4] disarmed, with a revenue of almost two millions sterling, at the mercy of our servants, who had adopted an unheard-of ruinous principle, of an interest distinct from that of the Company. This principle showed itself in laying their hands upon everything they did not deem the Company's property. To reform the abuses so described Clive invoked the assistance of those who ought to have been immediately concerned in the introduction of juster administration. He invited the young Nawáb and his councillors to Calcutta, and held with them long conferences. The disclosures which followed more than confirmed the worst fears he had entertained regarding the all but universal corruption of the members of the Civil Service. It was in consequence of these disclosures that he compelled the retirement from the Council, as he had found it composed on his arrival, of five of its members, and suspended the remaining three. He filled up the vacancies thus caused by indenting on Madras for a sufficient number of civilians to raise the total number of councillors to twelve.

[4] The word 'Súbah' is used here to mean one of the large divisions of the Mughal empire.

These sweeping reforms produced their natural effect. Clive became hated. The civilians and their friends and accomplices acted according as their natures were dominated by fear or by love of revenge. Of the former, one, greatly inculpated, the chief agent of Patná, committed suicide. Of the latter, many formed amongst themselves an association, of which the following were some of the principal articles:—'all visits to the Governor were forbidden; no invitations from him or from the members of the Select Committee were to be accepted; the gentlemen coming from Madras were to be treated with neglect and contempt; every member who should deviate from these rules would be denounced and avoided.' At a later period their hostility indicated itself in a more serious manner.

Of the young Súbahdár Clive formed but a poor opinion. He seemed to him a nullity. The one man of ability about him, the minister Muhammad Ríza Khán, the chief of those who had been bribed to raise him to the *masnad*, was absolutely without scruple. Clive was most unwilling to trust the political education of the Súbahdár to such a man, or to others about him who possessed his unscrupulousness but did not share his ability. But it was difficult to discover a better man; and Clive had ultimately to be content with the endeavour to lessen his influence by associating with him Rájá Duláb Rám—the general who had conspired with Mír Jafar before Plassey—and with the head of the great banking-house of the Sét family. But the influence of Ríza was too deeply founded to be lightly shaken.

The introduction of the reforms I have noted caused a great strain on the constitution of the illustrious man whose iron will carried them through. He had to fight against a faction of interested men, assailed by abuse, thwarted by opposition, and opposed secretly by at least one of the colleagues sent to support him. He was absolutely alone in the contest. But his brave heart and his resolute will carried him through. It was far more trying than fighting a battle, or planning and carrying through a campaign. In those cases there is always the excitement of constant action; the daily, often hourly, survey of the positions; the *certaminis gaudia* so eloquently described by Attila; 'the holiday,' as that great conqueror called it, 'of the battle-field.' In the daily examinations of deeds which call a blush to the cheek, and of devising measures to repress them in the future, Clive found none of these excitements. But though the work was dreary and heartrending, though, by reason of the opposition he encountered, it called into action all his mental vigour, all his intelligence, all his determination, it was terribly exhausting. It wore him out. Well might Sir John Malcolm write that it may be questioned 'whether any of Clive's many and great achievements called forth more of that active energy and calm firmness for which he was distinguished than was evinced in effecting the reform of the Civil Service of Bengal.'

There accompanied, moreover, in all his civil contests, another mental trial. From causes which have been stated none of the reforms, he constantly felt, could be stamped as 'thorough.' They were none of them complete. He did much; he broke down corruption; he laid the foundation for a permanent and perfect reform; he checked an enormous evil; he infused a healthier tone into the younger members of the service; he aided largely towards the rehabilitation of the British name, then sunk deep in the mire. But the want of intuition, of foresight, of the Court of Directors rendered it impossible for him to do more. That ultimate aim was to come after him; his principles were to triumph; his harassing work had not been done in vain. It was by adopting in their entirety the principles of Lord Clive that the Civil Service of India became one of the noblest services the world has ever seen, pure in its honour; devoted in the performance of its duties; conspicuous for its integrity and ability. It has produced men whose names would have given lustre to any administration in the world, and it continues to produce them still. The work of a great man lives after him. There is not a member of the Civil Service of India who does not realize that for them Clive did not live in vain.

Our admiration for him at this epoch of his career will be the greater when we realize that the administrative reforms I have mentioned were only a part of the duties which devolved upon him. Simultaneously with the dealing with them he had to devote his time and attention to other matters of the first importance. To the consideration of these I shall ask the reader's attention in the next chapter.

CHAPTER XIV
THE POLITICAL AND FOREIGN POLICY OF LORD CLIVE: HIS ARMY-ADMINISTRATION AND ITS CONSEQUENCES

On the 25th of June Clive started on his tour northward. His presence was urgently needed on the frontier, for he had to deal with two humiliated princes, the Nawáb-Wazír of Oudh, and the actual inheritor of the empire of the Mughal, Sháh Alím, now a houseless fugitive, his capital occupied by the Afgháns, possessing no resources but such as might accrue from the title which he bore.

At Murshidábád, which he took on his way upwards, Clive had to settle with the young Súbahdár the system which it would be incumbent upon him to introduce into the three provinces, as governor under the over-lordship of the English. The positions of the native ruler and the western foreigner had become completely inverted since the period, only nine years distant, when Siráj-ud-daulá marched against Calcutta to expel thence those who were his vassals. The system to be imposed now on the Súbahdár provided that he should become aNawáb-Názim, responsible for the peace and for the maintenance of public order in the three provinces, for the administration of justice, and for the enforcing of obedience to the law; that there should be a Diwán, or chief minister, empowered to collect the yearly revenue of the provinces, responsible for all disbursements, and for the payment of the surplus into the Imperial treasury. This system had prevailed in the time of the Emperor Aurangzeb. But there was this important difference. In Clive's scheme, whilst Nujm-ud-daulá would be Nawáb-Názim, the East India Company would occupy, from that time forth and for ever, the position of Diwán; and the Imperial treasury would be the treasury of the Company. The scheme was agreed to by the young Nawáb and his surroundings. But in working it, one part was found to place a power that would be abused in the hands of the Nawáb-Názim. Accordingly, a few months later, that prince was relieved of the responsibility for the maintenance of the public peace, for the administration of justice, and for the enforcing of obedience to the law. In a word, the Company became the rulers of the three provinces, the Nawáb-Názim a cypher. Nay, more, the sum of money which the Nawáb-Názim was to have at his disposal was limited to fifty-three lakhs of rupees; from this he was to defray the entire expenses of his court. Was it for such a result, might the shade of Mír Jafar inquire, that the nobles of the three provinces combined to betray Siráj-ud-daulá?

After having thus settled the affairs of the Company at Murshidábád, Clive proceeded by way of Patná to Benares, to meet there his friend General Carnac and the suppliant Nawáb-Wazír of Oudh. This interview was, in the eyes of Clive, likely to be fraught with the most important consequences, for he was bent on the securing of a frontier for the English possessions such as would offer the best points of defence against invasion; for, in his view, it was to be permanent.

It ought not to be attributed as a great political fault to Clive that his mind had not realized the fact that to maintain it is often necessary to advance. In a word, it would be most unfair to judge the action of 1765-6 by the lights of the experience of the century which followed. Up to the year 1757 the unwarlike inhabitants of Bengal had been the prey of the Mughal or the Marátha. But in 1765, so far as could be judged, neither was to be feared. The Marátha power had suffered in 1761, on the field of Pánípat, near Delhi, one of the most crushing defeats ever inflicted on a people, and Clive had no power of divining that the genius of a young member of one of their ruling families, who escaped wounded from the field, would, in a few years, raise the Marátha power to more than its pristine greatness. As for the Mughal, his power was gone for ever; the representative prince was at the very moment a fugitive at Allahábád, not possessed of a stiver. What was there to be feared from him or from his family? In the three provinces the English possessed the richest parts of India. It was surely good policy, he argued, if he could by treaty with his neighbours, and by occupying the salient points which covered them, render them unassailable.

After some preliminary conversation with the Nawáb-Wazír, Clive found that it would be necessary to proceed to Allahábád to confer there with the titular emperor, Sháh Alím. He found that prince full of ideas as to the possibility of recovering with the aid of Clive his lost possessions in the north-west. Nothing was further from Clive's mind than an enterprise of that character, and, with his accustomed tact he soon convinced the two princes that it was necessary first to settle the English frontier before discussing any other subject. He then proceeded to develop his plan. He demanded the cession of the fortress of Chanár to the English; the provinces of Karra and Allahábád to the Emperor, to be held, on his behalf, by the English; the payment by the Nawáb-Wazír of fifty lakhs, for the expenses of the war just concluded; an engagement from him never to employ or give protection to Mír Kásim or to Samru; permission to the East India Company to trade throughout his dominions, and to establish factories within them. The Nawáb-Wazír agreed to every clause except to that regarding the factories. He had observed, he stated, that whenever the English established a footing in a country, even though it were only by means of a commercial factory, they never budged from it; their countrymen followed them; and in the end they became masters of the place. He then pointed out how, in nine years, the small factory of Calcutta had absorbed the three provinces, and was now engaged in swallowing up places beyond their border. He would not, he finally declared, submit his dominions to the same chance. Recognizing his earnestness, and having really no desire to plant factories in Oudh, Clive wisely gave way on that one point. He carried, however, all the other points. It was further arranged that the Zamíndár of Benares, who had befriended the English during the war, should retain his possessions in subordination to the Nawáb-Wazír; that a treaty of mutual support should be signed between the English, the Nawáb-Wazír, and the Súbahdár of the three provinces; and that should English troops be required to fight for the defence of the Nawáb-Wazír's country, he should defray all their expenses.

Subsequently at Chaprá, in Bihár, Clive met the Nawáb-Wazír, the representative of Sháh Alím, agents from the Ját chiefs of Agra, and others from the Rohillá chiefs of Rohilkhand. The avowed purpose of the meeting was to form a league against Marátha aggression, it having been recently discovered that that people had entered into communications with Sháh Alím for the purpose of restoring him to his throne. Then it was that the question of the English frontier was discussed. It was eventually agreed that one entire brigade should occupy Allahábád, to protect that place and the adjoining district of Karra;[1] that a strong detachment of the second brigade should occupy Chanár; two battalions Benares; and one Lucknow. On his side the Emperor granted firmans bestowing the three provinces upon the East India Company 'as a free gift without the association of any other person,' subject to an annual payment to himself and successors of twenty-six lakhs of rupees, and to the condition that the Company should maintain an army for their defence.

[1] Karra was a very important division and city in the time of the Mughals, and is repeatedly referred to by the native historians whose records appear in Sir H. Elliot's history. See vols. ii, iii, iv, v and viii. The city is now in ruins.

On the 19th of May following the Súbahdár of the three provinces died. The arrangements made by Clive had deprived the position of all political importance. The individuality of the person holding that once important office was therefore of little importance. The next heir, a brother, naturally succeeded. The only change made on the occasion was the reduction of the allowance for all the expenses of the office from fifty-three to forty-one lakhs of rupees.

On one point Clive continued firm. Although, practically, the English had now become the masters of the three provinces, the Súbahdár only the show-figure, he insisted that the former should still remain in the background. The revenue was still to be collected in the name, and nominally on behalf of the native prince. The utmost he would permit in a contrary direction was to appoint English supervisors, to see that the native collectors did their duty. Beyond that he would not go. In the eyes of the world of India the three provinces were to continue a *Súbah,* administered by a Súbahdár. The control of the English was to remain a matter for arrangement with the actual ruler, their real power only to be prominently used when occasion might require, and then, likewise, in the name of the Súbahdár.

We have fortunately from his own hand the principles which guided him, and which he hoped would guide his successors, in their relations to the other powers of India. In a State paper[2] written before his departure, he thus expressed his views: 'Our possessions should be bounded by the provinces.' 'We should studiously maintain peace; it is the groundwork of our prosperity. Never consent to act offensively against any Powers except in defence of our own, the King's, or the Nawáb-Wazír's dominions, as stipulated by treaty; and, above all things, be assured that a march to Delhi would be not only a vain and fruitless project, but attended with destruction to your own army, and perhaps put a period to the very being of the Company in Bengal.' In a word, to borrow the criticism of the author from whose work I have quoted, 'the English were to lie snugly ensconced in the three provinces of Bengal, Bihár, and Orissa. The frontier of Oudh was to form a permanent barrier against all further progress.' Such a policy might commend itself to the theorist, but it was not fitted for the rough throes of an empire in dissolution, its several parts disputed by adventurers. Within a single decade it was blown to the winds.[3]

[2] *Early Records of British India,* by Talboys Wheeler. In this interesting work the paper quoted from is given *in extenso.*

[3] Wheeler.

There is one subject upon which it becomes me to touch slightly before considering the army administration. During one of his visits to Murshidábád it was discovered that, in his will, the late Súbahdár, Mír Jafar, had bequeathed five lakhs of rupees to Clive. The discovery was made after Clive, in common with the other servants of the Company, had bound himself not to accept any presents from natives of India. He could not therefore take the legacy himself. But the money was there—practically to be disposed of as he might direct. He resolved, with the approval of his Council, to constitute with it a fund for the relief of the officers and men of the Company's army who might be disabled by wounds or by the climate. Thus was formed the institution which, under the title of 'Lord Clive's Fund,' served to bring help and consolation to many poor and deserving servants of the Company for nearly a century. By a strange freak of fortune this fund reverted, in 1858, on the transfer of India to the Crown, to the descendants of the very man who could not, or believed he could not, accept it, when bequeathed to him, for himself.

Whilst dealing with the internal administration of the country, and arranging for the protection of its frontier, Clive had not been unmindful of the other duty strongly impressed upon him by the Court of Directors, that of examining the pay and allowances of their military officers, with special reference to an allowance known as Batta. Batta, in a military sense, represented the extra sum or allowance granted to soldiers when on field duty. Practically it had been granted on the following principle. Officers had been allowed a fixed monthly pay and allowances, not including batta, when they were serving in garrison. When they took the field they drew an extra sum as batta, known as full batta; but when they were detached to an out-station, not being actually in the field, they drew only half that amount, which was called half-batta. After the battle of Plassey, Mír Jafar, in the profusion of his gratitude, had bestowed upon the officers an additional sum equal to full batta. This was called 'double batta,' and as long as the army was in the field, fighting for the interests of that chief, he continued, with the sanction of the Council of Calcutta, to disburse that allowance. Mír Kásim, on his succession, had expressed his intention to continue this payment, and had assigned to the Company, for that purpose amongst others, the revenues of three districts. But the Court of Directors, not fully realizing that the transaction with Mír Kásim was one eminently advantageous to themselves, and forgetting that the receipt of the revenues of the three provinces was accompanied by an obligation, chose to forget the latter point, and accepting the revenues, issued peremptory orders to discontinue the disbursement of double batta. This order seemed so unjust that the then Council of Calcutta (1762), on receiving it, went thoroughly into the question, and, in a despatch to the Court, submitted the case for the officers in the strongest terms. The reply of the Court adds one proof to many of the unfitness of men not belonging to the ruling class to exercise supreme authority. The Directors refused the prayer of their servants on grounds which, by no artifice of despatch-writing, could be made to apply to the circumstances of the case.

That reply was dated the 9th of March, 1763. Just one month earlier the Calcutta Council had appointed a Special Committee on the spot to examine and report upon the question. But before the Committee could complete its inquiries there broke out that war with Mír Kásim, which called for the extraordinary exertions of the class whose claims were under examination. The services of Majors Adams and Carnac, two of the members of the Committee, were required in the field, and it was by the splendid exertions of the former and his officers that the Company was rescued from imminent peril. The inquiry dropped during the war.

But although the splendid exertions of the officers saved British interests in 1763, the Court of Directors did not the less persist in resolving to curtail their allowances. On the 1st of June, 1764, whilst the army, having conquered Mír Kásim, stood opposed to the forces of the Nawáb-Wazír of Oudh, they despatched the most precise orders that the allowance of double batta should be discontinued from the date of the receipt of their order. Probably the Court of Directors was the only ruling body in the world which would have dared to issue an order greatly curtailing allowances to an army in the field, opposed to greatly superior forces whose triumph would mean destruction to the Company. But this is but one instance of the dogged incapacity to rule with which the history of the Court of Directors abounds.

When the despatch reached India the army had but just gained the bloody and decisive battle of Baksar. The Calcutta Council dared not, at such a moment, carry out the orders of the Court. There were other reasons for delay. Lord Clive was on his way from England, and to him, probably, special instructions had been given.

We have seen the course which Lord Clive pursued with reference to the other branches of the administration. It was the end of the year 1765 before he touched the army. Then he issued instructions that from the 1st of January, 1766, the double batta should be withdrawn, except as regarded the second brigade, then stationed at Allahábád. This brigade, on account of the high prices of provisions at the station, and the expense of procuring the necessary supplies from Europe, was to be allowed double batta in the field, and the old original single batta in cantonments or in garrison, until it should be recalled within the provinces. This rule was to be applied to all troops beyond the Karmnásá. Clive directed further that the rest of the army should receive single batta when marching or in the field, and half single batta when in cantonment or in garrison, as at Mungír or Patná; but when at Calcutta or within the Presidency division the officers would receive no batta at all, but free quarters in lieu of it.

The order was badly received by the officers. They had enjoyed the privilege of double batta and its accessories so long that they had come to regard such allowances as their right by prescription. They at once memorialized the Government with a view to obtain a modification. But the reply Clive invariably gave them was to the effect that the orders of the Court had left him no option in the matter. Driven into a corner, their regard for their interests got the better of their sense of discipline. The officers of the several brigades and regiments entered into a correspondence with one another, formed committees, and decided to wrench by force the rights, as they deemed them, of which the order of the Court had deprived them. In a word, the European army of India, officers and men—for the men were prepared to follow the lead of the officers—combined against the Government.

Space will not permit me, nor is it requisite, that I should detail the measures they adopted to bend the Government to their will. It must suffice to state that the mutiny was of a most formidable character. So complete was the organization of the conspiring officers, so well laid were their plans, so secret had been their measures, that, during the period of four months the organization was in progress, not a single whisper of it had reached the Government. Clive received the first intimation of it when he was officially informed of it by the commander of the first brigade—a man who sympathized with the movement and desired its success. At the moment the conspirators were ready for action. That they possessed the sympathy of the members of the Civil Service was shown by the fact that the latter subscribed 140,000 rupees to aid the movement, and supplied the conspirators with copies of the proceedings of the Government.

Formidable as was the situation no living man was so well qualified to deal with it as was Clive. In the hour of danger he soared above his fellows. The danger here was greater than the danger of Arcot; than at the surprises of Káveripák and of Samiáveram; than during the hour of doubt at Plassey. His opponents were his own men—men whom he had led to victory. They possessed all the fortified places, the guns, the material of war. From the frontier came rumours of the advance of a Maráthá army, 60,000 strong, to wrest Allahábád and Karra from his hand. But there he was, the same cool, patient, defiant man he had been when confronted by the bayonets of the French at Káveripák and Samiáveram. He knew that the Government he represented was in the most imminent danger, that if the mutineers should move forward, he had not the means to oppose them.

The manner in which Clive met this danger is a lesson for all time. Not for an instant did he quail. Never was he more resolved to carry out the orders he had issued regarding batta than when he was told, that, in the presence of the enemy on the frontier, the officers would resign their commissions if the order were not withdrawn.

For the moment, fortunately, the conspirators had resolved to await his action. He, then, would take the initiative. On the very day when he received the report of the existence of the conspiracy he formed a committee, composed of himself, General Carnac, and Mr. Sykes, to carry out the plan of action he had formed. First, he and they resolved to send immediately to Madras for officers. Then they passed a resolution declaring that any officer resigning his commission should be debarred from serving the Company in any capacity, and sent copies of it to the several brigades for distribution to all concerned. Clive then hurried to Murshidábád; he addressed the recalcitrant officers stationed there; spoke to them in terms firm, yet conciliatory; told them they were acting very wrongly and very foolishly; that they were infringing the very discipline which they knew to be the mainstay of an army; that although immediate success might be theirs, they must be beaten in the long run; that such conduct could only be pardoned on condition of immediate submission. Touched by the language of the man who had been to them an object of veneration, all the officers, two young lieutenants excepted, hesitated—then submitted absolutely. This success was followed by similar results at the other stations in the Presidency division, visited by Carnac and Sykes. In that division only two captains and a lieutenant continued recalcitrant.

There remained then only the important centres of Mungír, Bánkípur (Patná), and Allahábád, the officers stationed there being bound to each other by the most solemn engagements. At the first-named of these places the Commandant was Sir Robert Fletcher, himself a well-wisher to the plot. When the officers there simultaneously tendered their resignation, agreeing to serve for fifteen days longer without pay, Fletcher received them with sympathy, and told them he would forward their letter to headquarters. At Bánkípur, then the military cantonment of Patná, the commandant, Sir R. Barker, one of the superior officers who had accompanied Clive from England, acted far differently. Before replying, he communicated with Lord Clive, then at Murshidábád, and received from him instructions to place under arrest every officer whose conduct should seem to him to come under the construction of mutiny, and to detain such at Bánkípur until it might be possible to convene a general court-martial to try them. To rendercomplete the necessary numbers of field-officers Clive promoted on the spot two officers known to be loyal. The Bánkípur officers followed, nevertheless, the conduct of their comrades at Mungír, and resigned in a body. Barker not only declined to accept those resignations, but arrested four of the ringleaders, and despatched them by water to Calcutta. This bold action paralyzed the recalcitrants, and followed up as it was by the journey of Clive to Mungír, accompanied by some officers who had come round from Madras, it dealt a blow to the mutineers from which they never completely rallied.

But at Allahábád the danger was still more menacing. There and at the station of Surájpur, only two officers, Colonel Smith, and a Major of the same name, were absolutely untainted: four were but slightly so, and could be depended upon to act with the Smiths in an emergency; all the others had pledged themselves to 'the cause.' Those of the latter stationed at Allahábád displayed their disaffection in the usual manner, whereupon Major Smith, commanding there, calling on the sipáhís to support him, placed under arrest every officer in the place, the four slightly tainted officers excepted. He then informed the mutinous officers that he would shoot down without mercy any and every officer who should break his arrest. This action was most effective. All the officers but six submitted and were allowed to return to duty. The six were deported to Patná, to be tried there. A similar course was followed by Colonel Smith atSurájpur, with the result, however, that nearly one half of the officers remained recalcitrant, and were despatched under arrest to Calcutta.

Meanwhile, at Mungír, the officers continued in a thorough state of disorganization, the commander, Sir Robert Fletcher, encouraging them. The day before Clive's arrival, an officer whom he had sent in advance, Colonel Champion, surprising the officers in full conclave, learned from them that they desired to recount their grievances to Clive in person. On learning this Clive directed them to parade with their men the following morning, giving directions simultaneously to Champion, to bring to the ground two battalions of sipáhís, under the command of Captain F. Smith, an officer known to be loyal. Then a very curious circumstance happened. Smith had but just entered the fort with his sipáhís when he noticed that the Europeans, infantry and artillery, were turning out to mutiny. Without a moment's hesitation he marched towards them with his sipáhís; seized, by a bold strategic movement, a mound which was the key of the position, completely dominating the ground on which the Europeans were drawn up. The latter, who were on the point of quitting the fort, noting the commanding position occupied by the sipáhís, halted and hesitated. Smith took advantage of the pause thus caused to tell them that unless they should retire instantly to their barracks he would fire upon them. At the moment Sir R. Fletcher came up, began to encourage the revolters, and to distribute money amongst them; suddenly, however, taking in the exact position, he changed his tone, ordered the recalcitrant officers to leave the fort within two hours, and reported the whole circumstance to Lord Clive. The officers left at once, and the incident closed for the day; but when, the following morning, Clive entered the fort, and addressed the assembled soldiers on the wickedness of their conduct, praised and rewarded the sipáhís for their behaviour, the men gave way. The mutiny, as far as Mungír was concerned, was over. Meanwhile the officers expelled by Fletcher had encamped within a short distance of Mungír, resolved to wait there the arrival of their comrades from other stations. But they had to deal with a man who would stand no trifling. Clive despatched to them an order to set out forthwith for Calcutta; and to quicken their movements he sent a detachment of sipáhís to see that his order was obeyed. After that there was no more mutiny at Mungír, or in the stations dependent upon it.

At Bánkípur the officers, notwithstanding the action of Sir R. Barker, previously noted, had sent their commissions *en bloc* to Lord Clive. But the news of the occurrences at Mungír startled and frightened them. When, then, Lord Clive arrived at Patná, he found the officers penitent and humble, and that his only task was to pardon. There, too, he learned with pleasure the successful action of the two Smiths at Allahábád and Surájpur. He remained then at Patná, to crush the last embers of the mutiny, and to arrange for the bringing to justice of the ringleaders. This last task he performed in a manner which tempered justice with mercy. Fletcher, who had played a double part, and whose actions were prompted by personal greed, was brought to a court-martial and cashiered. Five other officers were deported, but of these, one, John Neville Parker, was reinstated in 1769, and survived to render glorious service to the Company, giving his life for his masters in 1781.

The comparative ease with which Clive suppressed this formidable conspiracy was due to one cause alone. No sooner did Clive hear of the combination than, instead of waiting to be attacked, he seized the initiative: the mutineers allowed him to strike the first blow; standing on the defensive in their isolated positions, they gave the opportunity to Clive to destroy them in detail. It was the action which Napoleon employed against the Austrians in 1796, 1805, and in 1809. It is useless to speculate what might have been the result if Clive had stood, as the majority of men would have stood, on the defensive. By the opposite course he not only saved the situation, but achieving a very decisive victory, struck a blow at insubordination which gave an altered tone to the officers of the army, then as much hankering after ungodly pelf as were their brethren in the Civil Service. Never, throughout his glorious career as a soldier, did Clive's character and his conduct stand higher than when, in dealing out punishment for the mutiny which he, and he alone, had suppressed, he remembered the former services of the soldiers who had been led away, and gave them all, a few incorrigibles excepted, the opportunity to retrieve their characters on future fields of battle.

The task of Clive in India had now been accomplished. Thoroughly had he carried through the mission entrusted to him. He had cleansed, as far as was possible, the Augean stable. He had given himself no recreation: he was completely worn out. He had announced to the Court of Directors so far back as 1765 his intention to resign as soon as he could do so without inconvenience to the public interests. The Court, in reply, whilst most handsomely acknowledging his services, had begged him to devote yet one year to India. When that letter reached him, December 1766, he had already accomplished all that, with the means and powers at his disposal, it was possible to carry through. He felt then that, broken in health, he might retire with honour from the country he had won for England. Having penned a valuable minute, laying down the principles which should guide the policy of his successor, based upon his own action during the preceding three years, he made over to one of his colleagues of the Select Committee, Mr. Verelst,[4] the office of Governor, and nominating Colonel Richard Smith, then on the frontier, to be Commander-in-chief, Mr. Sykes, Mr. Carter, and Mr. Beecher, to form, with the Governor, the Select Committee, he bade farewell to his friends, and, on the 29th of January, 1767, embarked on board the good ship *Britannia* for England.

[4] Mr. Sumner, whose weak character I have described, and who had been designated Lord Clive's successor, had been forced to resign his seat on the Select Committee.

CHAPTER XV
THE RETURN OF THE CONQUEROR-STATESMAN, AND THE RECEPTION ACCORDED TO HIM BY HIS COUNTRYMEN: HIS STRUGGLES; AND HIS DEATH

One of the ablest and most impartial of English historians, the fifth Earl Stanhope, has thus summed up his appreciation of the results of the second administration of Clive in India: 'On the whole it may be said that his second command was not less important for reform than his first had been for conquest. By this the foundations, at least, of good government were securely laid. And the results would have been greater still could Clive have remained longer at his post.' It was impossible he could remain. In December, 1766, his weakness was so great as to disable him from writing. He required rest, and as we have seen he embarked for England at the close of the month following, to find there, alas! no rest, but, on the contrary, the bitterest, the most persistent, the most unscrupulous enemies; their attacks prompted by the corrupt officials whom he had driven from the posts they had abused, and who were able, nevertheless, to enlist in their vile persecution statesmen of great renown holding high office under the Crown.

It is a pitiful tale, this persecution of a man who had rendered the most magnificent services to his country. The one blot minute investigation had been able to find in his career was the treatment of Aminchand. But Aminchand was a blackmailer who had threatened to betray a state-secret of enormous importance unless he were paid a sum out of all proportion to the services he rendered. Such a man deserves no commiseration. His treachery, if Clive had refused to subscribe to his terms, would have involved the death of thousands, and might have driven the English out of Bengal. Clive fought him with the same Asiatic weapon Aminchand had levelled against himself, and beat him. That his action was wrong in morals, unworthy of his lofty nature, is unquestionable. But it is not so certain that, under similar pressure, in circumstances so critical, those who most bitterly denounced him would have acted otherwise. Some writers have averred, and until recently it has been accepted, that the deceit drove Aminchand to madness. But inquiry has dissipated this fiction. He was, it is true, startled into insensibility by the discovery of the fact that he had been imposed upon, but, after visiting the shrine of a famous saint in Málwá, he returned to his business in Calcutta and prospered till his death. As to the other part of the same transaction, the signing of the name of Admiral Watson, Clive stated on oath, in his evidence before the House of Commons, that although the admiral had refused to sign the document, he had, to the best of his belief, permitted Mr. Lushington to affix his name; and certainly amongst those who benefited by the transaction was Admiral Watson himself, who, after the triumph of the conspirators, claimed even more than he received. But it was on these two points that the miscreants whom Clive, in his second administration, had driven from the posts they had sullied, and their allies, based a persecution which tortured the enfeebled frame of the conqueror.

Clive's real fault in the eyes of the leaders of the persecution was that he had become rich himself, and had prevented them from fattening on the plunder of the country he had conquered. To most men, in fact to all but a very few men, in England and in France, India was a *terra incognita* whither a certain few repaired young, and whence they returned, in the prime of their manhood, rich, and often with a great reputation. Why was it that such men were at once subjected to the vilest persecution? The fact that they were so is incontestable. Clive himself and Warren Hastings, whose reputation has recently been splendidly vindicated by two great Englishmen,[1] are cases in point in England; Dupleix and La Bourdonnais and Lally, in France. It is the saddest of sad stories; the men who had rendered the most brilliant services to their respective countries finding their bitterest enemies often amongst the Ministers of the Crown. There is little to discriminate between the conduct of parliamentary England and despotic France except in the degree of misery and punishment to which they alike subjected the most illustrious of their countrymen who had served in India.

[1] Sir Fitzjames Stephen in the case of Nanda-Kumár: Sir John Strachey in reference to the charges respecting Oudh and Rohilkhand.

To return. It will be remembered that in his second administration Clive had purified the Civil Service of Bengal. The corrupt men whom he had ejected had returned to England whilst he was still in India, the charges made against them accompanying or preceding them in the despatches transmitted to the Court of Directors. On receiving these despatches the Court, having taken the opinions of their own lawyers and of those of the Crown, resolved to bring the culprits to trial for having accepted presents from the natives after they had received the order from the Court making such acceptance penal. But the inculpated men were rich and they resolved to appeal from the Directors to the Proprietors. There had been a difference between these two bodies as to whether the annual dividends should be increased from ten, the amount recommended by the Court, to twelve and a half per cent. At the annual meeting the votes of the men dismissed by Clive enabled the Proprietors to carry their point. The corrupt clique utilized this victory by proposing and carrying a resolution that the prosecutions instituted against them should be dismissed. This was accordingly done.

Two months later, July 14, Clive landed in England. He was well received. The King and Queen admitted him to private audiences. The Court of Directors received him in full conclave, immediately after his reception by their Majesties, thanked him for his splendid achievements, and immediately convened a general Court to confirm the proposal that the jágír, granted him by Mír Jafar, should be confirmed to him for an additional ten years. This resolution was unanimously passed.

So far there was no sign of the coming storm. Not a sound of the distant hurricane had been wafted to the ears of Clive. He had returned as ambitious as he ever had been, resolved to devote to the service of his country the energies he had displayed in the East. Already he had made arrangements to secure seats for himself and for six of his relatives, when, to rest before the elections should take place, he started for Paris (January, 1768) with Lady Clive and a small party. He was very confident in the future. He had received personally the King's commands to lay before his Majesty his ideas of the Company's affairs both at home and abroad, with a promise of his Majesty's countenance and protection in anything he might attempt for the good of the nation and the Company. He had seen so much of what he called 'the ignorance and obstinacy' of the Court of Directors, who, he stated in a letter to his successor, Mr. Verelst, 'are universally despised and hated,' that he felt sure his would be the hand, in the coming meeting of the Court of Proprietors, to stay their fall or to renew their vitality. In a word, his confidence was never greater, never did he feel more assured regarding the future.

Yet, during this confidence of the soul, this longing for political warfare, his nearest friends could easily detect that he had not sufficiently recovered from the strain of his last three years in India. His body did not respond to the call of the ever active brain. His friends and his physicians urged him then to take a complete rest and holiday of fourteen to fifteen months in France. With difficulty they induced him to stay eight months. Then he returned to find that he and his six relatives had, in his absence, been elected Members of Parliament.

His return produced a renewal of the activity of his enemies. They filled London with stories of his rapacity. Sir Robert Fletcher, whose shameful conduct during the mutiny of the officers I have recorded, wrote against him a pamphlet which irritated him greatly. He was hardly to be prevented from answering it. There were other considerations which, at this time, affected his career. When the general election at which he and his friends were returned had taken place, the Ministry was presided over by the Duke of Grafton, Lord Chatham being Lord Privy Seal and Lord North Chancellor of the Exchequer. At the end of 1769 Chatham was forced by the state of his health, which had long been bad, to resign; and in the January of the year following, the Duke of Grafton resigned and was succeeded as First Lord of the Treasury by Lord North. Clive had not posed as a supporter of either of these administrations. He had declared himself to be a supporter of George Grenville, the head of the Grenville Whigs, who were then in opposition. It has been claimed[2] for him that Clive declined to commit himself to any party of the Indian policy of which he was ignorant. But none of the members of Lord North's Cabinet knew anything of India, and if Clive, commanding seven votes, had been asked to join it, he might have educated his colleagues on the subject. An opportunity of following such a course seemed to occur when Mr. Wedderburn, an able lawyer and a personal ally of Clive, joined the North Ministry, but Clive remained staunch to the Grenville connexion, exercising but little influence, and exposed all the time to the bitter shafts of his enemies, which increased every day in intensity and venom. To make the situation still less endurable George Grenville died (November, 1770).

[2] Malcolm's *Clive*.

Meanwhile affairs in India were not progressing satisfactorily. In Bengal, indeed, Mr. Verelst, acting on the lines laid down by Clive, had with the support of his colleagues succeeded in maintaining peace and prosperity. But in Madras, the incursions of Haidar Alí, an adventurer who by sheer ability and daring had climbed to the highest place in the kingdom of Mysore, had caused the English in that Presidency severe losses, and forced them to incur an expenditure which deprived the Proprietors of Indian Stock of all chance of dividends for some time to come. To meet this financial embarrassment the Crown and the Company could dream of no other device than the futile one of sending to India three commissioners, who, under the name of Supervisors, should have full power over all the other servants of the Company. They nominated accordingly Mr. Vansittart, who, from having been the warmest friend of Clive, had become his bitterest opponent; and who, but for the successful opposition of Clive and his friends, would have been appointed Governor in succession to Mr. Verelst. With him they associated Mr. Scrafton, an old and valued servant of the Company; and Colonel Forde, the conqueror of the Northern Sirkárs and of Biderra—both intimate friends and adherents of Clive. These gentlemen sailed in the *Aurora* frigate in the autumn of 1769. The *Aurora* reached the Cape in safety, but was never heard of after she had quitted Simon's Bay. It was supposed that she foundered at sea.

Some considerable time elapsed before it had been realized in England that the Supervisors had failed them, and that it would be necessary to take other measures to remedy existing evils. Meanwhile events had happened which increased the necessity for immediate and effective action. In 1770 the three provinces were visited by a famine exceeding in intensity all the famines of preceding ages. There had been, in years gone by, no beneficent strangers from the West to make, as in later years, provision for the occurrence of so great a calamity. The rains had failed; the water in the tanks had dried up; the rice-fields had become parched and dry. There were but few stores handy to enable the foreigner to disburse the necessary grain. It was the first famine-experience of the English, and they too had made no provision for it. The misery was terrible. The large centres of industry, the only places where there was a chance of obtaining food, became thronged with the dying and the dead. The rivers floating corpses to the sea became so tainted that the very fish ceased to be wholesome food. In summing up, two years later, the effects of the famine on the population, the Governor-General in Council declared that in some places one-half, and, on the whole, one-third of the inhabitants had been destroyed. It need scarcely be added that this terrible calamity affected the Proprietors of East India Stock in a manner, to them the most vital:—it destroyed their prospects of large dividends.

To remedy this evil the brains of the Court of Directors could devise no other scheme than that which the foundering of the *Aurora* had previously baffled: they would send out other Supervisors. But Lord North had taken the matter in hand. He brought in a bill providing for the constitution in Calcutta of a Supreme Court, to consist of a Chief Justice and three Puisné judges, appointed by the Crown; giving to the Governor of Bengal authority over the two other Presidencies, with the title of Governor-General, to be assisted and controlled by a Council of five members. The great blot of this bill was the clause which gave a controlling power to the Council. The Governor-General had in it but one vote, and in case of equality, a casting-vote. Mr. Warren Hastings who, twelve months before, had succeeded Mr. John Cartier[3] as Governor, was appointed first Governor-General of India.

[3] Mr. Cartier had succeeded Mr. Verelst in 1769.

The war with Haidar Alí and the famine in Bengal had brought India and Indian matters very prominently into the parliamentary discussions of 1771, 1772 and 1773, and during these the name of Lord Clive had not been spared. The attacks against him were led principally by General Burgoyne, a natural son of Lord Bingley, best known in history as the commander who surrendered a British army, 5,791 strong, to the American colonists.[4] In April, 1772, this officer had become Chairman of a Select Committee composed of thirty-one members, to inquire and report on Indian affairs. Another Committee, called Secret, and composed of thirteen members nominated by ballot, was appointed, on the motion of Lord North, in November of the same year, to take into consideration the whole state of the Company's affairs. Into the other proceedings of these committees this volume has no cause to enter; but they had scarcely been constituted when they began to let fly their arrows at Lord Clive. The chief cause of these attacks is so well stated by the sober-minded historian,[5] that I cannot refrain from quoting his remarks. 'Besides the public wrongs of which he (Lord Clive) stood accused, there was also, it may be feared, a feeling of personal envy at work against him. His vast wealth became a more striking mark for calumny when contrasted with the financial embarrassments of the Directors in whose service he had gained it. And his profusion, as ever happens, offended far more persons than it pleased. He had bought the noble seat of Claremont from the Duchess Dowager of Newcastle, and was improving it at lavish cost. He had so far invested money in the smaller boroughs that he could reckon on bringing into Parliament a retinue of six or seven friends or kinsmen. Under such circumstances the Select Committee, over which Burgoyne presided, made Clive their more especial object of attack. They drew forth into the light of day several transactions certainly not well formed to bear it, as the forgery of Admiral Watson's signature, and the fraud practised on Aminchand. But at the same time they could not shut out the lustre of the great deeds he had performed. Clive himself was unsparingly questioned, and treated with slight regard. As he complains, in one of his speeches: "I their humble servant, the Baron of Plassey, have been examined by the Select Committee more like a sheep-stealer than a member of this House." And he adds, with perfect truth: "I am sure, Sir, if I had any sore places about me, they would have been found: they have probed me to the bottom; no lenient plasters have been applied to heal; no, Sir, they were all of the blister kind, prepared with Spanish flies and other provocatives."'

[4] At Saratoga, October 17, 1777.
[5] Lord Stanhope's *History of England*, vol. vii. pp. 353-4.

Throughout these attacks Clive never lost his calmness or his presence of mind. Never once did his lofty spirit quail. He stood there still the unconquered hero, ready to meet every charge, sometimes retorting, but always nobly, on his adversaries. His friends rallied gallantly round him. His particular friend, Mr. Wedderburn, then Solicitor-General, gave him a support as valuable as it was unstinted. When his administration in Bengal was spoken of by his old enemy, Mr. Sulivan, in the House in a manner which, whilst not directly attacking it, conveyed the impression that there was a great deal more in the background, Clive went through every phase of his career in Bengal, defending his own action in a style which gained for him admiration. It was not, however, until the month of May, 1773, that General Burgoyne defined the vague charges which had theretofore supplied the place of argument, and brought them forward, as a vote of censure, in three resolutions. These resolutions ran as follows: (1) 'that all acquisitions made under the influence of a military force, or by treaty with foreign princes, did of right belong to the State'; (2) 'that to appropriate acquisitions so made to the private emoluments of persons entrusted with any civil or military power of the State is illegal'; (3) 'that very great sums of money, and other valuable property, had been acquired in Bengal from princes and others of that country by persons entrusted with the civil and military powers of the State by means of such powers; which sums of money and valuable property have been appropriated to the private use of such persons.'

These resolutions named nobody. But in the speech in which they were introduced Burgoyne took care that there should be no doubt as to the person against whom they were directed. He dwelt, with a bitterness not to be surpassed, on all the delinquencies, real and imaginary, of the conqueror of Bengal. He traced all the misfortunes which had subsequently happened to the Company to the treasonable compact which had dethroned Siráj-ud-daulá and placed Mír Jafar on his seat, and denounced the conduct of the authors of that transaction as 'black perfidy.' He denounced, also, in terms equally severe, the treatment of Aminchand; the forging of the name of Admiral Watson; the agreement, which, he said, had extorted from Mír Jafar enormous sums, under the guise of presents, to the leading servants of the Company in Bengal. On the second administration of Clive, which was really a long struggle against the corruption by which he was surrounded, Burgoyne railed as bitterly and as unsparingly. Nor was he content with merely railing. Before he sat down he declared that if the House should pass his resolutions he would not stop there, but would proceed to follow them up with others, hisobject being to compel those who had acquired large sums of money in the manner he had denounced to make a full and complete restitution.

The Solicitor-General, Wedderburn, conducted the defence for Clive, and it was noticeable that the party styled 'the King's Friends,' amongst many others, gave him their support. The Attorney-General, Thurlow, supported Burgoyne, and the Prime Minister, Lord North, voted with him. The voting on these resolutions did not, however, indicate the real sense of the House, for many of those who supported them thought it would be better for the cause of Clive that the further resolutions threatened by Burgoyne should be proceded with in order that a decisive vote should be taken on a motion implicating Clive by name rather than on resolutions of a vague and general character. The resolutions, then, were carried.

Burgoyne then proceeded, as he had promised, to follow up his victory. On the 17th of May he brought forward the following resolution: 'That it appears to this House that the Right Honourable Robert, Lord Clive, Baron of Plassey, in the kingdom of Ireland, about the time of the deposition of Siráj-ud-daulá, and the establishment of Mír Jafar on the *masnad*, through the influence of the powers with which he was entrusted as member of the Select Committee and Commander-in-chief of the British forces, did obtain and possess himself of two lakhs of rupees as Commander-in-chief, a further sum of two lakhs and eighty thousand rupees as member of the Select Committee, and a further sum of sixteen lakhs or more, under the denomination of a private donation, which sums, amounting together to twenty lakhs and eighty thousand rupees, were of value, in English money, of two hundred and thirty-four thousand pounds; and that in so doing the said Robert Clive abused the power with which he was entrusted, to the evil example of the servants of the public, and to the dishonour and detriment of the State.'

No one could say that these charges were not sufficiently pointed. Clive met them with his accustomed resolution. He rejoiced that the real issue had come at last; that the great jury of the nation, the House of Commons, was, after so long an interval devoted to calumny, to abuse, to vague and shadowy charges, to record its vote on the real question. On their decision on this resolution he would stand or fall. The alternative which his fiercest fights had presented to him, the necessity to conquer or to be disgraced, was presented to him here. He had won those fights by the exercise rather of his lofty moral qualities than by his skill as a soldier, and by the exercise of the same qualities he would win this one also. And he did win it. After Burgoyne, introducing his resolution, had traversed the same ground he had followed in the preceding resolutions, and had concluded by calling upon the House, like the old Roman heroes, 'to strike when the justice of the State requires it,' Clive rose to defend himself. Recapitulating the services he had rendered, he reminded the House that the transactions in Bengal, upon which Burgoyne relied for a conviction, had been known in their general tenour to the Company and the Crown when they had thanked him, not once but repeatedly, for his services. He proceeded then to expose the interested and revengeful motives of the clique which had instigated the attack, not sparing even those in high places who, from various causes, had allowed themselves to sanction it. Turning from that point, he asked prominent attention to the fact that the India Office, now his accuser, had almost forced him to proceed for the second time to Bengal, and had expressed a deep regret that his health had not allowed him to stay there longer. 'After certificates such as these,' he added, 'am I to be brought here like a criminal, and the very best parts of my conduct construed into crimes against the State?' Stating then that the resolution, if carried, would reduce him to depend on his paternal inheritance of £500 per annum, he continued: 'But on this I am content to live; and perhaps I shall find more real content of mind and happiness than in the trembling affluence of an unsettled fortune. But, Sir, I must make one more observation. If the definition of the hon. gentleman (Colonel Burgoyne) and of this House, that the State, as expressed in these resolutions, is, *quoad hoc*, the Company, then, Sir, every farthing I enjoy is granted to me. But to be called upon, after sixteen years have elapsed, to account for my conduct in this manner, and after an uninterrupted enjoyment of my property, to be questioned, and considered as obtaining it unwarrantably, is hard indeed; it is a treatment I should not think the British Senate capable of. But if such should be the case, I have a conscious innocence within me that tells me my conduct is irreproachable. *Frangas non flectes*.[6] My enemies may take from me what I have; they may, as they think, make me poor, but I shall be happy. I mean not this as my defence, though I have done for the present. My defence will be heard at that bar, but before I sit down I have one request to make to this House: that when they come to decide upon my honour, they will not forget their own.'

[6] 'You may break, but you shall not bend, me.'

The debate was adjourned, and in the few days following some witnesses gave evidence at the bar of the House. Lord Clive's evidence, given before the Select Committee, was also read there. In the debate that followed, Mr. Stanley proposed to omit the words inculpating the honour of Clive. Mr. Fuller seconded this amendment, going even further, and striking out the sentence referring to the exercise of undue influence. His suggestion was accepted, and the House proceeded to discuss the amendment as so altered. After a protracted debate the division was called for, when it was found that 155 members had voted for the amendment and 95 against it. This victory stripped Burgoyne's resolutions of all their sting. Vainly did a member of his party attempt to restore the battle by moving that Clive had abused the powers intrusted to him in acting as he avowedly had acted. The House refused to re-open that question. Finally, at five o'clock in the morning, the House passed the following resolution, which consummated the defeat of Burgoyne: "That Robert, Lord Clive, did, at the same time, render great and meritorious services to his country.' On this conclusion to the violent attacks on Clive, Lord Stanhope, well versed in Parliamentary procedure, thus wrote: 'Such a vote might be deemed almost a verdict of acquittal. Certainly, at least, it showed a wise reluctance to condemn. It closed the whole case, and Clive had no further Parliamentary attack to fear.'

But though the victory was gained, the struggle affecting the personal honour and fortune of a proud and sensitive man had made deep inroads upon the constitution of one who had been long suffering from the acute agony caused by the malady contracted in India. Freed from the attack of his enemies, he might, had his health been only tolerable, have looked forward to a high command in the war just about to break out with the colonists of North America. There he would have been in his place; there, under the influence of constant action, he would have forgotten his troubles; even his oft-recurring spasms might have disappeared. But, after the Parliamentary contest was over, with the waning of the ever-present excitement, his health became worse. In vain did he repair to Bath to try the effect of its waters. In vain, finding that for him the virtues of the Bath waters had departed, did he proceed to the Continent for travel. Rest came not. A complication of disorders prevented sleep, and travel failed to remedy the evil. His mind had no longer the sustaining power which in former days had enabled him to meet with tranquillity the frowns of Fortune. He returned to England in 1774, and shortly afterwards, in November of that year, when apparently thoroughly conscious,[7] fell by his own hand. "To the last,' wrote Lord Stanhope, 'he appears to have retained his serene demeanour and stern dominion of his will.' It is difficult for us who have followed his career to realise the terrible upsetting of the balance of the great brain which had brought such an act within the bounds of possibility.

[7] Lord Stanhope relates a story regarding the manner of Clive's death, told by the Earl of Shelburne, afterwards the first Marquis of Lansdowne, to the person from whom he (Lord Stanhope) received it. 'It so chanced, that a young lady, an attached friend of his (Clive's) family, was then upon a visit at his house in Berkeley Square, and sat writing a letter, in one of its apartments. Seeing Lord Clive walk through, she called him to come and mend her pen. Lord Clive obeyed her summons, and taking out his penknife fulfilled her request; after which, passing on to another chamber, he turned the same knife against himself.'

'Such was the end,' says a French writer, 'of one of the men who did the most for the greatness of England.' That foreign verdict is at least incontestable. Caesar conquered Gaul for his country; Hannibal caused unrest to Rome for nearly a quarter of a century; Wellington drove the French from Portugal and Spain. The achievement of Clive was more splendid than any one of these. He founded for this little island in the Atlantic a magnificent empire; an empire famous in antiquity, renowned since the time of Alexander, whose greatest sovereign had been the contemporary of Queen Elizabeth, more enlightened than any of her predecessors, more tolerant, a more far-sighted statesman even than she. He was, according to Lord Stanhope, emphatically 'a great man.' But he was more than a great man. Like Caius Julius, he united two personalities; he was a great statesman and a great soldier. He was a man of thought as well as a man of action. No administration surpasses, in the strength of will of the administrator, in excellence of design, in thoroughness of purpose, and, as far as his masters would permit, in thoroughness of action, his second administration of Bengal. No general who ever fought displayed greater calmness in danger, more coolness of brain, than did Clive at Káveripák, at Samiáveram, at Calcutta, when, on the fog rising, he found himself enveloped by the Súbahdár's army, 40,000 strong. Nothing daunted him; nothing clouded his judgement; his decision, the decision of the moment, was always right. In a word, he was a born master of men.

But, says the moralist, he committed faults, and at once the false treaty made with Aminchand is thrown into the face of the historian. Yes, he did do it; and not only that, he stated in his evidence before the House of Commons that if he were again under the same circumstances he would do it again. None of his detractors had had the opportunity of judging of the terrible issues which the threatened treachery of Aminchand had opened to his vision. Upon the decision of Clive rested the lives of thousands. To save those lives there appeared to him but one sure method available, and that was to deceive the deceiver. I think his decision was a wrong one, but it should always be remembered that, as Clive stated before the Committee, he had no interested motive in doing what he did do; he did it with the design of disappointing a rapacious man and of preventing the consequences of his treachery. He was in a position of terrible responsibility, and he acted to save others. Let the stern moralist stand in the same position as that in which Clive stood, and it is just possible he might think as Clive thought. At all events, this one fault, for fault it was, cannot or ought not to be set up as a counterweight against services which have given this island the highest position amongst all the nations of the earth. The House of Commons, after a long debate, condoned it. Might not Posterity, the Posterity which has profited by that very fault, be content to follow the lead of the House of Commons? With all his faults, Clive was 'one of the men who did the most for the greatness of England.' That fact is before us every day. His one fault hastened his death, from the handle it gave to the envious and the revengeful, and took from him the chance of gaining fresh laurels in America. May not the ever-living fact of his services induce us to overlook, to blot out from the memory, that one mistake, which he so bitterly expiated in his lifetime?

Printed in Great Britain
by Amazon